DISCOURSE AND PSYCHOLOGY

This book presents a unique understanding of the interdependence between language and psychology and how one's speech is shaped by and in turn shapes one's thoughts, beliefs, and emotions. Drawing on the tenets of discourse analysis and psychology, it presents a comprehensive guide to a new and burgeoning area in linguistics and critical theory. The volume focusses on individual and group behaviour to show how identity formation is as much dependent on the psychological state as on social surroundings and context. It introduces various concepts from the sociocognitive framework, discursive and critical psychology, highlighting the myriad ways of approaching the complex interface between text, sociocultural factors, and cognitive processes.

An indispensable guide to the complex world of language and the unconscious, the volume will be of interest to students and scholars of linguistics, applied linguistics, sociolinguistics, psychology and behavioural science, language, and critical theory. It is also a must-read for the general reader interested in language, communication, and social intelligence.

Saumya Sharma is Assistant Professor (Linguistics) at the English and Foreign Languages University, Lucknow Campus, India. She was a guest faculty member at the Indian Institute of Technology Kanpur for a year, where she taught a course on composition and communication skills. Her research interests include examining the discourse-psychology interface, particularly gender issues, vocabulary teaching, and critical pedagogy. She has published in the areas of English-language teaching, stylistics, and critical discourse analysis. Some of her recent publications include *Language, Gender and Ideology: Constructions of Femininity for Marriage* (Routledge, 2018) and *Common Errors in Everyday English* (2017).

DISCOURSE AND PSYCHOLOGY

An Introduction

Saumya Sharma

Routledge
Taylor & Francis Group
LONDON AND NEW YORK

First published 2020
by Routledge
2 Park Square, Milton Park, Abingdon, Oxon OX14 4RN

and by Routledge
52 Vanderbilt Avenue, New York, NY 10017

Routledge is an imprint of the Taylor & Francis Group, an informa business

© 2020 Saumya Sharma

The right of Saumya Sharma to be identified as author of this work has been asserted by her in accordance with sections 77 and 78 of the Copyright, Designs and Patents Act 1988.

All rights reserved. No part of this book may be reprinted or reproduced or utilised in any form or by any electronic, mechanical, or other means, now known or hereafter invented, including photocopying and recording, or in any information storage or retrieval system, without permission in writing from the publishers.

Trademark notice: Product or corporate names may be trademarks or registered trademarks, and are used only for identification and explanation without intent to infringe.

British Library Cataloguing-in-Publication Data
A catalogue record for this book is available from the British Library

Library of Congress Cataloging-in-Publication Data
A catalog record for this book has been requested

ISBN: 978-1-138-09068-2 (hbk)
ISBN: 978-0-367-34795-6 (pbk)
ISBN: 978-0-429-34232-5 (ebk)

Typeset in Bembo
by Apex CoVantage, LLC

 Printed in the United Kingdom
by Henry Ling Limited

To those who taught me that the beads of language are strung on the thread of psyche, shaping society

CONTENTS

	Introduction	1
1	Discourse: history and meanings	3
2	Sociocognitive approaches	17
3	Discourse and action	36
4	Discourse, repertoires and out-there-ness	49
5	Rhetoric and ideological dilemmas	63
6	Psychosocial studies and critical psychology	74
7	Analysis	91
8	Conclusion	107
	Weblinks	*112*
	Bibliography	*114*
	Index	*127*

INTRODUCTION

This book is a primer to the vast yet engaging area of discourse and psychology, and the idea for writing it germinated in my attempts to find answers to the following questions. How can an individual's discourse(s) be related to how they think and feel? To what extent and in what ways is language an indicator of one's psychological state? And can a person's identity be constructed both socially and psychologically? While doing research to relate these questions, I realised that there is no single answer but many answers, depending on how one is approaching the topic and how discourse is understood and defined in one's study. This work, therefore, introduces the reader to the multiple ways in which one's language and psychology can be explored. Since a lot of research already exists in the broad areas of language, cognitive psychology and psycholinguistics, drawing on concepts from each other, I have not dealt with those areas. In comparison, I use language in the discursive sense, and my work exclusively focusses on the meanings of discourse and the interrelationships between discourse and psychology. It describes how psychologists understand and use discourse in psychology to explore human behaviour, and how discourse analysts have employed psychological concepts to examine the links between discourse, power and society. It also explains the use of discourse by psychoanalysts to investigate the intersections of the social and psychological dimensions, and wherever possible, attempts have been made to highlight how identities are constructed through the complex matrix of discourse, psychology, power and ideology as many practitioners have examined the operations of power and/or ideology in human relations and society at large. The book, therefore, is interdisciplinary in focus, delving on several issues and highlighting that human subjectivity is myriad and richly textured.

Since several notions are proposed by the theorists and they themselves belong to different areas, it became important to explain each person's perspective to avoid conceptual confusion. Thus, each chapter introduces one or more approach

2 Introduction

and its related themes and issues. The work describes and maps in detail the major theoretical strategies, salient concepts, methodologies and critical debates as proposed and developed by theorists in discourse analysis, discursive psychology, psychosocial studies and critical psychology. The primary focus is on the seminal research of each scholar and what they have to say about their perspective; however, research by others is also discussed to emphasise how a concept has been utilised. Since the discursive thread binds each of the different perspectives, the chapters have been arranged according to the use of discourse in each approach, beginning with discourse studies and moving towards psychology and psychoanalysis. In the process I have not only traced the history and development of discourse analysis and its various meanings, but also how the meaning of discourse has been extended and modified by researchers from other disciplines.

In addition, brief sample analyses have been given drawing on concepts from the approaches discussed, demonstrating their practical applications for students, researchers and teachers. An attempt has been made to include the fundamentally significant ideas of each approach; thus every chapter can either be read separately as a self-contained unit, or sequentially as part of the book. Since the book provides a bird's-eye view of the inextricable and subtle links between discourse and psychology, suggested reading is given at the end of each chapter to facilitate in-depth understanding of topics, and weblinks have also been listed at the end of the book for further research in areas that might arouse the reader's interest. This book can benefit not only students and teachers of discourse analysis, psychology and psychoanalysis but even those in media studies, gender and sociology if their work is broadly concerned with an exploration of how individuals are shaped psychologically, socially and linguistically.

This introduction would not be complete without my giving credit to those who have contributed directly and indirectly to the creation of this work. I would like to thank my family for their unconditional love and support while I wrote this book. Special thanks to Aakash Chakrabarty and Brinda Sen for their keen interest in this project. I also express my heartfelt indebtedness to Professor Rajneesh Arora, Ms. Mira Yog, Dr. Manjul Pande Parvez and Ms. Kavita Agarwal who made discourse and psychology very interesting and lively areas of study. While writing the book, I read a lot of literary fiction and spiritual literature that portrayed the complex interplay between language, society and psyche, and I'm extremely grateful for the inspiration that such writings provided.

1
DISCOURSE
History and meanings

Discourse analysis: an introduction

In the past four decades, owing to the 'discursive turn' in the social sciences, discourse analysis has established itself as an interdisciplinary area that focusses on the use of language and its analysis, in sociocultural contexts. Derived from the Latin word *discursus* meaning 'running to and fro,' the word 'discourse' was used for the first time in the treatise *Discourse on Method* (1637/2006) by the Italian philosopher René Descartes (1596–1650). In common parlance, discourse can be treated both as a noun and a verb. As a noun it refers to the multiple discourses that create the social world, and as a verb it denotes the act of creating these discourses. This chapter deals with two areas fundamental to discourse: the development of discourse analysis as an academic area that has provided the tools and concepts in discourse, and the various linguistic and social meanings of discourse. An understanding of discourse is essential before we proceed to examine the use of the term by different theorists, especially psychologists, which forms the major part of this book.

Origins of discourse analysis

The development of discourse analysis does not follow a linear path. Rather, it *dis-courses*, evolving from such diverse terrains as Saussure's structuralism to sociolinguistics and pragmatics. According to Teun A. van Dijk (1985), the origins of discourse analysis can be traced back 2,000 years ago to classical *rhetorica* and *grammatica* practiced by the Greeks and Romans. The emphasis in both these disciplines on norms for language use, the organisation and presentation of public speech and the persuasive power of language to bring about an attitudinal change in the audience, anticipated contemporary discourse analysis, highlighting that just as psychology was relevant for oratory, discourse analysis too relied on

4 Discourse

several psychological concepts for understanding a text such as memory, cognition, schema, point of view, etc. However, major developments in discourse took place in the twentieth century with growth in structuralism, semiotics, narratology and anthropology (van Dijk 1985) that indirectly helped in maturation of the discipline by showing that a text, its contexts and culture were constructed and understood through discourse. It needs to be pointed that the works produced in these areas did not explicitly describe discourse, but they provided the base for larger textual analysis in literature, culture, media and social interaction. Thus, the term 'text' in those days, like the present times, broadly meant speech and writing in any area. This was significant for at that time, in linguistics, Chomskyan grammar was in vogue much to the neglect of language analysis beyond the sentence, and so the earlier studies provided a major impetus to the field of discourse. Propp's *Morphology of the Folktale* (1968) was one of the initial structural studies on discourse of folktales. Simultaneously, influenced by semiotics, extensive work on culture and myths (Strauss 1963) brought about developments in anthropology. The publication of articles on semiotic and narrative analysis by such eminent linguists and literary critics as Roland Barthes, A. J. Greimas, Gerard Genette and Umberto Eco shifted attention to larger discourse chunks and structural interrelations between them. Barthes gave a meticulous critique of advertising, entertainment and the signs of consumer culture in his book *Mythologies* (1972), while Genette and Greimas discussed the concept and types of narratives in their works on narrative discourse (1980) and structural semantics (1983) respectively. These prolific writers, though differing in orientation and methodology, made a concerted effort at analysing discourse or language within the larger sphere of semiotic, literary and linguistic interpretation.

In the 1960s and 1970s, owing to trans-Atlantic studies, discourse analysis emerged as a separate discipline with its sub-branches, sharing its theoretical orientation with pragmatics, sociolinguistics and grammar. One form of discourse analysis, that is, narrative analysis – the study of discoursal features of narratives and storytelling – was done in both speech and writing. Studies in this direction were undertaken by the renowned sociolinguist William Labov (1966, 1972) who analysed forms of verbal duelling and ritual insults in the oral narratives of African-American adolescents in New York City as an indicator of class and status. Before him, Dell Hymes (1972, 1974), a professor of anthropology, published his views on language, society and speech patterns that later developed into the field of ethnography of communication. Laying emphasis on the situational nature of speech, Hymes proposed the mnemonic SPEAKING for analysing language in context: the cultural and psychological setting (S), participants (P), public and private outcomes known as ends (E), message form and content referred to as act sequences (A), tone of speech known as key (K), instrumentalities or channels of speech (I), norms of production and interpretation (N) and genres (G). About a decade later, Goffman (1981) elaborated on the microanalysis of face-to-face encounters between people and how they negotiated their identities, while Gumperz (1972, 1999) studied intercultural interaction among

Discourse 5

various groups along with the mechanisms that lead to misinterpretation, be it a nod, a word, a differing intonation or any such occurrence. His methodology was later known as interactional sociolinguistics. In the 1980s M. A. K. Halliday propounded his theory of systemic functional linguistics (SFL) that viewed language as an interrelated system of sounds and words as well as sentences. Halliday (1994) proposed that meaning making depended on the choices of the speakers/ writers, accentuating their intentionality. This feature was later used by critical discourse analysts (Fairclough 1989) to highlight the use of language in larger social contexts and its interaction with social/political ideologies and power play.

Intercontinental pragmatics was another area that provided an impetus for the analysis of discourse because many theories in discourse analysis, in fact, came from pragmatics. One of the earliest was speech act theory (Austin 1962; Searle 1969, 1979) which saw language as performing action on the basis of which one could accomplish things. Thus, language use was contextualised, motivated and varied; that is, it could be spoken in many ways to show one's intentions, beliefs and evaluations about the environment. These theorists provided a classification of speech acts under the categories of illocutions (the force of an utterance) and per-locutions (their effects on the hearers). For example, thanking, ordering, greeting and promising were all speech acts that, when spoken in particular contexts, produced particular effects on the listeners. The sincerity of the speaker together with the appropriacy of the context and conditions (sincerity and felicity conditions) were also significant for talk and therefore analysis. Similarly, H. P. Grice, a philosopher and the exponent of the theory of implicature, argued in his classic paper 'Logic and Conversation' (1975/2008) the concept of the cooperative principle and its maxims as the underlying basis for conversation. Interested in the questions of truth, falsity, logic and reference, Grice stated that in day-to-day talk people were governed by conversational maxims of quantity (speak as much as is required), quality (truthfulness), relation (relevance) and manner (brevity) in an attempt to carry out clear and harmonious conversation, and that violations of these maxims caused implicature, indicating that the speaker wanted to convey more than what was said. Grice's influence was seen in the theories of linguistic politeness (Brown and Levinson 1987) and relevance (Sperber and Wilson 1986). The former dealt with strategies of politeness in communication, the latter with the notion of relevance in talk. The theory of politeness, in particular, was extremely influential in understanding the way in which people communicated using politeness strategies. Brown and Levinson (1987) proposed the concept of 'face' as possessing two dimensions: our desire to be appreciated and liked by people (positive face) and our desire to not be imposed upon (negative face) by others. Politeness strategies varied depending on the extent to which they maintained or threatened one's face. In recent years, the strategies of impoliteness (Culpeper 2011) have been developed as an extension and a contrast to politeness to indicate why and how people speak aggressively.

Apart from pragmatics, the study of grammar too became a vital part of discourse. Grammar was no longer viewed in terms of a strict structural analysis

6 Discourse

of sentences (Harris 1952), but it became the subject of extensive research in the interdisciplinary sphere of text linguistics and discourse. Concepts such as cohesion and coherence, topic, comment, presupposition, overall semantic structures and features of texts were employed by Robert-Alain de Beaugrande and Wolfgang U. Dressler (1981) and M. A. K. Halliday and Ruqaiya Hasan (1976) to highlight the ways in which grammatical and textual features created multiple discourses and points of view and often a rearrangement of words could altogether create a different world. Simultaneously, attention was paid to the formal, systematic study of everyday conversation by ethnomethodologists or conversation analysts Harold Garfinkel (1967), Aaron Cicourel (1973), Harvey Sacks, Emanuel Schegloff, and Gail Jefferson (1974) and Erving Goffman (1981). How people talk by taking turns, manage the topic and the floor, give preferred and dispreferred responses to others, repair one's speech and maintain silence were some of the topics under study. This sociological approach to talk was extremely useful in understanding any kind of conversation, be it telephonic, institutional, literary, political, social, medical, etc., and many penetrating insights were gained through the detailed study of hitherto 'mundane' talk. A variation of this approach was found in Sinclair and Coulthard's (1975) study of classroom discourse which delved on the initiating, responding and feedback moves made by students and teachers in an attempt to create, understand and negotiate meanings in context. These discourse analysts argued for rigorous practices in the observation and interpretation of interaction at the micro-level in various contexts, emphasising the shift from a grammatical analysis of language to its use, choice and function in larger contexts.

The theories of pragmatics and systemic functional grammar provided valuable tools for scrutinising discourse particularly in a critical manner, giving rise to critical linguistics and critical discourse analysis. Critical discourse analysis (CDA) is a crucial branch of discourse studies that built on the work of critical linguists who were interested in examining ideology in language use. Unlike the earlier approaches in discourse that were descriptive and non-critical – for instance, speech acts, politeness, conversation analysis and implicature – CDA seeks to understand the role of ideological processes and power relations in the construction of social reality through analysing the relation between texts, discourse and society. The play of ideology and power can be deciphered textually and contextually in literary texts (Fowler 1977, 1981; Fowler et al. 1979), and/or in institutional settings such as the workplace, classrooms, hospitals and bureaucracy, as exemplified in the works of Norman Fairclough (1992, 1993, 1995a, 1995b, 2003) and Ruth Wodak (1991, 1996, 1997) and Wodak and Matouschek (1993) and in socio-psychological phenomena as prejudice and racism (van Dijk 1985, 1987, 1991a, 1998, 2008a, 2008b). This approach sees "language as a form of social practice" where there exists a dialectical relationship between language and society (Fairclough 1989: 22). The approach is interdisciplinary, depending upon the theoretical orientation of the practitioner; however, in all its forms it attempts to highlight inequalities and discrimination, thus becoming a mode to increase critical language awareness (Fairclough 1992) in the community.

Discourse analysis in linguistics has also been appropriated in other areas, one of them being psychology which is the focal point of this book. These developments in discourse analysis were concomitant with those in discursive psychology, an umbrella term for different psychologists who have incorporated discourse in their works. Discursive psychology (Billig 2009), now an established branch in psychology, emerged as a reaction against traditional psychological emphasis on statistical procedures and experimental methods whereby humans were treated as cases. Jonathan Potter and Margaret Wetherell's *Discourse and Social Psychology: Beyond Attitudes and Behaviour* (1987) was a landmark critique of the existing methodology and assumptions in social psychology. They argued for a re-examination of beliefs, assumptions and values, taking context into account and not relying solely on the decontextualised self-reported attitudes of people. John Shotter's book *Conversational Realities* (1993), like that of Potter and Wetherell, enunciated the problem of variation versus consistency in social sciences. Following Edward Sapir and Benjamin Lee Whorf's hypothesis on linguistic relativity, Shotter proposed a rethinking of the processes through which we construct our reality, both social and cultural. He explored the significance and pervasiveness of descriptions and factual accounts in our lives, how they are produced to appear objective and neutral, independent of the speaker's personal views and what speakers do by producing such descriptions – in other words, how descriptions are actional and the psychological work that goes into producing them. Yet another approach to discursive psychology was that of Michael Billig (1991, 1996) who proposed a detailed study of rhetoric, particularly in politics, by developing an argumentative approach based on the discourse of the Greco-Roman writers, asserting that the way people constructed their arguments could be an indicator of their ideological and political beliefs. Though each approach in discursive psychology varied, a few commonalities can be gleaned. Concepts such as memory, schemas, scripts and frames were employed in understanding texts and discourses (van Dijk 1985). Often, discourse was used in the performative sense by discursive psychologists, and attention was given to how individuals created meaning through their spoken discourses. Discursive psychologists insisted upon the need to seek out variance in the study of any social phenomena rather than conform to the notions of stability and uniformity sought after by earlier psychologists. Individuals were viewed as sentient and cognitive beings who transformed their surroundings in the way they spoke about it: what they saw, what they reacted to, how they understood people and events, and how they expressed their emotions, beliefs, views and values in words, etc. A person's psyche was not embedded in discourse but operated in and through discourse.

In addition to the earlier approaches, other practitioners provide critical psychological readings. Ian Parker (2015a) dissects individuals and events through the lens of power, ideology and discourse, focussing on how people are simultaneously constrained and enabled in social settings. A similar view is held by

8 Discourse

Emerson and Frosh (2004), who rely on a critical narrative (discursive) analysis of social phenomenon, employing Lacanian vocabulary to understand how people mediate and create their identities interpersonally and socially. Thus, discursive psychology that began by using concepts from social psychology (scripts, schemas, memory) has expanded to include a critical perspective just as CDA theorists added a critical dimension to discourse analysis. However, a word of caution is that each approach in discourse analysis and in discursive psychology has differing orientation, using discourse in a distinctive sense, and the use of one or more approaches requires careful consideration and reflexive thinking. Moreover, though psychologists have used discourse and given it new meanings, a similar approach towards psychological concepts is not found among discourse analysts who tend to be wary of the psyche, restricting themselves to spoken or written discourse. This book, therefore, attempts to delineate the approaches of those discourse analysts who have included psychological concepts in their understanding of social behaviour and those psychologists who have discursively analysed the speech of individuals in social and cultural contexts.

Meanings of discourse

Though the 'discursive turn' in the social sciences can be attributed to the 1960s, there are no unanimously agreed-upon definitions of discourse. In this brief overview I will primarily discuss the linguistic and critical meanings of discourse. Its use by psychologists constitutes the remainder of the book. The dictionary meaning of the term discourse refers to written or spoken communication (Oxford Dictionary), yet the word has multiple meanings across disciplines. In linguistics itself, 'discourse' has been defined and understood in many ways by theorists showing their varied focus and orientation. One of the earliest attempts at defining discourse, in linguistics, was by Zellig Harris (1952) who explained that discourse was not the study of isolated morphemes and random bits of sentences but the interrelationship between sentences to form a coherent whole. However, his approach was rudimentary and structural, a distributional analysis that aimed to find the meanings of formal features associated with particular discourses and their correlation with particular situations. Although he did not explore language use in society, his contribution seems historically significant because it was an explicit attempt at investigating connected discourse.

The term discourse is often contrasted with the related terms of text and sentence, and the differentiation between them might throw further light on the meanings of discourse. Crystal provides a broad yet very basic perspective that discourse focusses on "the structure of naturally occurring spoken language" but text analysis "focusses on the structure of written language" (1987: 116); however, such a distinction is untenable since nowadays both written texts and spoken conversations are analysed as 'texts' using discourse analytic tools. It follows that discourse(s) can be present in any text, and we perhaps need a more

Discourse **9**

nuanced explanation for further contrast. The view of H. G. Widdowson, I feel, is quite useful here:

> Texts come in all shapes and sizes: they can correspond in extent with any linguistic unit: letter, sound, word, sentence, combination of sentences . . . But identifying something as a text is not the same as interpreting it. You may recognize intentionality but not know the intention. This is where discourse comes in, and why it needs to be distinguished from a text . . . Discourse in this view is the pragmatic process of meaning negotiation. Text is its product.
>
> *(Widdowson 2004: 8)*

A text is a linguistic unit that can be understood only through discourse, by relating the words in a text to the extralinguistic reality (context) and actively finding meaning in the text. We can say that discourses can be read off texts, which consist of sentences. Semantically, a sentence is understood as a string of words grammatically put together (Hurford, Heasley and Smith 2007), and sentences create connected speech/writing which can be discursively understood. That is the reason why Michael Stubbs defines discourse as analysis above the sentence; even though he does not distinguish between discourse and texts, he writes that discourse "attempts to study the organization of language above the sentence, or above the clause, and therefore to study larger linguistic units, such as conversational exchanges or written texts" (1983: 2). Stubbs provides a broader and more inclusive understanding of connected speech and writing as discourse. However, his view is limited in the semiotic sense because a text can include visuals, actions and images; therefore texts can be verbal and visual, having one or more discourses. Texts can be read and seen, so it is better to refer to their authors as text creators or producers. Besides the difference between text and discourse, other analysts have explained discourse in functional terms as the study of language usage:

> the analysis of discourse is, necessarily, the analysis of language in use. As such, it cannot be restricted to the description of linguistic forms independent of the purposes or functions, which those forms are designed to serve in human affairs.
>
> *(Brown and Yule, 1983: 1)*

Brown and Yule's definition is relevant because it does not focus on the medium of language but on what constitutes discourse and how it is actional in nature. This definition brings us to the significant notion of 'doing' discourse in everyday context, a fundamental feature of theories of pragmatics that overlap with discourse. A similar functional account can be found in Hallidayan grammar where a text performs various functions: textual (the meanings encoded in a text), experiential (the knowledge about the world and belief

10 Discourse

system) and interpersonal. A text can be spoken or written but is a set of sentences encoded with meaning, while the job of the discourse analyst is to discover those meanings (Halliday and Matthiessen 2014). Analysis pays attention to the use of cohesive markers (repetition, substitution, ellipsis, conjunction and lexical cohesion) that provide surface-level connectedness, which in turn helps to understand a text globally and coherently (Halliday and Hasan 1976). Functional perspectives on discourse view language as multi-dimensional and choice-based, throwing light on the intentionality of the speaker; and in this sense they are more specific than the earlier definitions, yet they do not focus on how discourse intersects with social issues of race, class, gender and power and how discourse is related to cognition, an aspect we will return to later. The interaction of the functional perspective with the critical would be helpful in understanding language and discourse as multi-layered, nuanced and constructed in social contexts, as found in the recent studies of language and gender (Holmes and Meyerhoff 2003).

Two more notions of discourse emerge in terms of pragmatic meaning. Discourse arises through what is unsaid; the meanings conveyed in everyday talk are more than what is textually written as found in the theory of implicature (Grice 1975). The discourse of the producer is governed by his knowledge of the world, social beliefs, assumptions and values that can vary from those of the reader/ hearer. Therefore, in defining and understanding discourse, one needs to give attention to the divergence and the inferential processes in interpreting the text. Discourse can also be defined in terms of exchange structure and conversation structure. These are large chunks of talk between speakers who negotiate and create meaning. Discourse is conceptualised as a hierarchical pattern consisting of transactions in descending order: lesson, transaction, exchange, move and act corresponding to paragraph, sentence and smaller grammatical units. "Exchanges combine to form transactions and it seems probable that there will also be a number of transaction types . . . the highest unit of classroom discourse, consisting of one or more transactions, we call *lesson*" (Sinclair and Coulthard, 1975: 22–23, emphasis original). Discourse becomes dialogic characterised by turns taken by the interlocutors to complete a conversation such as question-answer-feedback or accusation-account-evaluation (Cody and McLaughlin 1985). In pragmatic and conversational terms, discourse is again viewed as performative action, highlighting how meanings are produced yet speech is multi-layered and socially constituted, inhabited by the indices of class, race and gender which need to be critically explored. Therefore, the functional and pragmatic views of discourse would become more textured if discourse is understood in a wider sociopolitical sense. Critical analysts have employed such a lens.

Discourse can be understood in a much wider sociocultural sense as a symbolic activity. James Paul Gee argues that "language is used in tandem with action, interactions, non-linguistic symbol systems, objects, tools, technologies, and distinctive ways of thinking, valuing, feeling and believing . . . language-in-action is always and everywhere an active building process" (2005: 10). For him, discourse is

Discourse **11**

a form of social action arising from people's way of living, acting and their use of technology in different contexts. The definition by Gee amalgamates the earlier views of doing or practising discourse along with the creation and enactment of identities and networks through discourse. The perspective is quite exhaustive for it is verbal, semiotic and sociopolitical in its implications. Gee draws a useful link between language and society in the following way: "When 'little d' discourse (language-in-use) is melded integrally with non-language 'stuff' to enact specific identities and activities, then I say that 'big D' Discourses are involved" (2005: 7). Discourse, thus, becomes mediated and negotiated action referred to as Discourse (in capital letters), while the use of language which is an integral part of this, but not synonymous to it, is known as discourse (in small letters). However, Gee too does not focus much on cognition and critical theory.

A similar view is held by CDA theorists who understand discourse as social practice where a dialectical relation exists between discourse and non-discursive institutions. For instance, the language of medicine is interrelated to the institution of hospitals and clinics. Even though CDA has different versions because of the varied theoretical orientation of analysts, all agree that language is exploited by dominant groups for maintaining their power and ideology. Fairclough and Wodak, two prominent theorists, state that:

> Discourse is socially constitutive as well as socially shaped: it constitutes situations, objects of knowledge, and the social identities of and relationships between people and groups of people . . . Discursive practices may have major ideological effects: that is, they can help produce and reproduce unequal power relations.
>
> *(1997: 258)*

For CDA practitioners, like Gee, speech and actions constitute discourse, producing knowledge about individuals and the world, but the focus is on representation and misrepresentation through language that accentuates the perpetuation or transformation of ideologies in society, together with relations of dominance and control. In fact, critical linguists like Roger Fowler (1981) rightly believe that language is an ideological conduit that can be exposed through a detailed reading of the text using tools from systemic functional grammar as seen in his extensive work on analysis of newspapers. Thus, discourse analytic tools from earlier approaches can be successfully employed with a critical perspective. The CDA approach is one of the most comprehensive and nuanced, allowing the analyst an eclectic but methodical selection of discourse tools and concepts for the analysis. Moreover, the emphasis is on how social categories function through discourse and talk, acknowledging that language use is complex and varied; but apart from van Dijk, most CDA practitioners do not focus on cognition and other psychological states, even though individuals are to a large extent governed by their thoughts, opinions, emotions and attitudes while speaking and writing. A perspective on discourse that takes the critical and psychological aspects

12 Discourse

into consideration would in actuality explain the operation of the intersecting currents of social norms and individual psyche, in all its complexity. In short, we do discourse, reflecting our race, gender, ideology and our thoughts and emotions. However, researchers need to be self-reflexive in understanding this conception of discourse and in navigating through what is 'critical' and what is 'psychological.'

Apart from linguists who engage in the study of language use, the thinker whose use of the term 'discourse' has had far-reaching implications is Foucault. Although, in his view, discourse is the means of manifesting and understanding the network of power relations in society, his use of the term is relatively abstract and social, unlike linguists who focus on verbal language. Foucault describes discourse in his classic work *Archeology of Knowledge* as:

> Whenever one can describe, between a number of statements, such a system of dispersion, whenever, between objects, types of statement, concepts, or thematic choices, one can define a regularity (an order, correlations, positions and functionings, transformations), we will say, for the sake of convenience, that we are dealing with a discursive formation.
>
> *(1972/2010: 41)*

Discourse does not limit itself to an analysis of verbal statements but also includes sociocultural and sociohistorical variables that occur at particular time periods, creating certain forms of truth or power. The analysis of statements includes all kinds of texts (verbal, visual, sociocultural and historical) that highlight the cultural construction of discourse and its socially constitutive nature. The attempt is to find patterns of regularity and irregularities; the normative patterns, the veiled truths and the blind spots for a particular discursive formation. However, discourse does not function in a vacuum but through individuals, social institutions and practices, which means an examination of individuals' speech is crucial to understanding their roles in a particular discursive formation. What people speak or write, from which positions they do so, to whom they are addressed and how they create objects of knowledge – these are some of the critical questions that Foucault puts together under the umbrella term 'enunciative modalities.' Such social roles act as conduits for the distribution and reproduction of power relations in society. Foucault's classic example on the construction of madness and the birth of psychopathology underscores the role of the doctor, policemen, witnesses and patient in classifying, dissecting and analysing information about insanity and the insane, and in maintaining the power arrangements in Western society in the seventeenth century.

Moreover, a particular discursive formation can be understood through discursive strategies, within and without, through the internal relations that exist in one or more discourses: analogy, complementarity, contrast, linearity, intertextuality, presence, absence, continuity, discontinuity, concomitance, etc. Such intertextual and intratextual relations indicate how and why discourses

Discourse **13**

become what they are, what they are composed of and their role in a discursive formation. For instance, an examination of dowry deaths in the 1990s would focus on the social and historical texts that produced knowledge on dowry deaths such as newspapers, documentaries, films, social commentaries, historical data, institutional records (hospital, legal and police), etc. The analysis needs to explore several facets of the problem. How are the victims and the perpetrators represented? Through what means does dowry death become the object of knowledge, and what is the role of society in perpetuating such actions? How are dowry deaths defined, described and contrasted with other forms of violence? What is the comparison between the data of the 1990s and that of earlier times? What are the links to other texts on dowry from different disciplines? These are some of the questions that can be examined as part of the analysis, the aim of which would be to uncover hitherto opaque power relations in society. Foucault's understanding of discourse is markedly different from its use in linguistics, where the focus is on language. However, his powerful yet abstract social concepts can be concretised through attention to language, bridging the gap between critical theory and language as in the works of critical discourse analysts (see Fairclough 1989). Other theorists, like Bakhtin (1994), provide a different meaning to discourse, not just as a vehicle for communication but as dialogicity – the creation of meaning through the utterances of the speakers that are chronologically related to each other and to other utterances within that context and other contexts, producing a view of discourse as intertextual and deferred. Such a view can work in tandem with the critical perspective to show the multiplicity of voices existing in a discourse and how these voices serve as conduits of power and ideology.

The concept of discourse, therefore, includes the following notions:

1   It ranges from the lexical to sentential level.
2   The use of language in the context (social, educational, economic and political) and the meanings which arise from it – that is, what the participants say and do not say – contribute to meaning formation.
3   Inferences and/or interpretation regarding meaning and intention are different from the perspective of the speaker and hearer, writer and reader (in case of a literary text), and hence never neutral or 'natural.' Moreover, interpretation takes place through verbal and non-verbal means.
4   Language is produced to perform certain functions (interpersonal, ideational and textual as stated by Halliday); therefore, discourse analysis covers the functional analysis of language in a way.
5   Discourse views language as a medium invested with power and ideology. Consequently, a study of discourse at the micro-level is a study of how society works at the macro-level (Jaworski and Coupland 1999).
6   Discourse is a carrier for our opinions, beliefs, attitudes and emotions, an area that needs more attention in discourse studies.

14 Discourse

The investigation of discourse is called discourse analysis and the area of study is known as discourse studies. Broadly, it refers to the examination of the relationship between form and function in language. But, as found in the discussion of the term 'discourse,' there are divergent views regarding the approach 'discourse analysis,' depending on which of the above-mentioned aspects form the focus of study, the sentence, the function, the meaning, the social/political or a combination of all these. In such a case, discourse analysis becomes very wide, overlapping with pragmatics and sociolinguistics, encompassing different methods of analysis from these fields.

A crucial understanding of discourse is in cognitive terms where information is implied or presupposed in a text that requires the activation of background knowledge to understand the text. For instance, the statement 'cabin lights will be dimmed on take-off and landing' requires knowledge of air travel and aeroplanes. The use of the word cognition refers to social cognitive concepts such as memory, schema, metaphors, attitudes and beliefs, highlighting how people think and act cognitively to produce discourse and also how language use requires fundamental cognitive concepts for understanding the world around us. Thus, the meaning of discourse needs to be elaborated to include this view. The next chapter will discuss some approaches in this regard. Since the concept of cognition is widely used in language sciences, and that too in more than one way, it is important to note that in this book, cognition is not viewed in the psycholinguistic sense and/or mentalist paradigm where language learning is a cognitive skill, but in the social-psychological sense of how individuals create and negotiate their identities using discourse, and how their psychological states are operationalised through their discourses.

Scope of discourse analysis

Discourse studies is an exhaustive area, spanning various topics and fields of inquiry as theoretical linguistics, pragmatics, psychology, anthropology and sociology. In each of these, the focus is different, ranging from study of everyday conversation, speech acts and speech events to the psychological and ideological basis of discourse; yet in each, discourse is considered "language use relative to social, political and cultural formations – it is language reflecting social order but also language shaping social order and shaping individuals' interaction with society" (Jaworski and Coupland, 1999: 3). It is multimodal and multi-layered, covering vocal, verbal and non-verbal communication such as written and oral texts, painting, sculpture, architecture, body language, music, film and so on. Discourse analysis can be local and/or general, depending on the objectives of the investigator. Its qualitative orientation ensures salient insights into language use and society, and its study of both the spoken and written medium has wider scope for systematic research in several fields such as law, medicine, therapeutic discourse, literature, films, newspapers, language processing and now even corpus linguistics that can be used as a quantitative tool to the analysis of discourse,

Discourse **15**

particularly over a large corpora that cannot be subjected to detailed, rigorous analysis. Popularly known as Corpus-assisted discourse studies (CADS), it involves the examination of corpora, including the techniques of key words, word cluster frequency lists and concordance, to look at the tokens of discourse (the number of times and the ways in which particular words occur) that can confirm, support or refute qualitative analysis, providing both a wider overview and a detailed picture of the phenomenon under research. These techniques are gradually gaining popularity in CDA (Baker 2014; Halloran 2014).

In almost all approaches on discourse analysis, context is a relevant analytical category, and therefore it needs to be explained here and distinguished from co-text. Co-text refers to the words surrounding a particular word, phrase or group of sentences within a text that help in understanding the meaning of that specific word/text. Co-textual meaning is largely linguistic in nature, pertaining to what occurs before and after a word or sentence that can throw light on its meaning. Context, in contrast, is a more general term whose meanings lie outside the text, referring to the background knowledge or situation that helps to understand the text. Context creates talk or language and vice versa, providing the scaffold for the text. In discourse studies, context can be used in a narrow sense to refer to the language used by speakers to create and negotiate meaning, or it can include broader, social categories such as gender, race, power, economic status, etc., to expand the meanings of a conversation. In the analysis of written texts, these social indices become the extra-textual on the basis of which the text is understood. Each discourse analyst and psychologist uses the term in his/her own way, making it a multi-layered concept. An example can clarify these statements. In Keats's *La Belle Dame Sans Merci*, the words that surround the phrase 'knight-at-arms' constitute the co-text for the phrase, while the contextual meaning arises because of the imagery, thematic structure, literary style and background to the poem and age.

This book is divided into different chapters that explain and demystify the work of discourse analysts and psychologists who have employed the term discourse in their research, enhancing the study of both language and psychology, since the speech and writing of individuals can be better understood through their emotions, attitudes and other psychological states. The focus of this book is the mapping of the basic assumptions and principal tenets in seminal approaches to discourse and psychology, comparing and contrasting them whenever possible. This book is a critical introduction in two ways. Firstly, some theorists have explicitly or implicitly used the notions of power and ideology, an examination of which is included in this work. Secondly, an overall assessment of the approaches is provided, apart from their practical applications in the chapter on analysis.

Summing up

The study of discourse analysis does not follow a linear trajectory. Beginning with literary/narrative studies and semiotics, discourse became a full-fledged

16 Discourse

discipline within linguistics and was later appropriated to other areas like psychology. The orientation of the researchers and their methodological perspective varies, yet the fundamental concern in examining discourse is how language works and what language does at multiple levels. Initially developed as the study of meaning above the clause, discourse studies make use of varied theories and concepts from functional grammar, politeness and conversational sequences, to critical concepts of power and ideology that enable one to understand meaning in context. The often-neglected but crucial aspect of social cognition is yet another insightful dimension of discourse. Both the co-text and the context are relevant for the analysis of discourse.

Suggested reading

Teun A. van Dijk's (1985) introduction to discourse analysis as a new cross-discipline charts the development of discourse in linguistics and allied areas. Jaworski and Coupland's (1999) introduction in the *Discourse Reader* briefly explains the various theoretical approaches to discourse, including discursive psychology. Schiffrin's (1994) work on the theoretical approaches to discourse analysis is a more advanced and nuanced guide, while Paltridge (2006) provides a comprehensive description of discourse and its related notions in a lucid, reader-friendly manner. So does Johnstone (2008) in her introduction to discourse analysis.

2
SOCIOCOGNITIVE APPROACHES

Introduction

Critical discourse analysis is exemplified mainly through the works of Fairclough (1992, 2003), Wodak (1991, 1996, 1997), van Dijk (1998, 2009) and Leeuwen (2004). Since the focus is on unravelling power relations and ideological assumptions through language, most CDA practitioners avoid the use of cognition and psychological states in their research paradigm and analysis. Fairclough, for instance, lists the use of schemas in his toolkit for interpretation, categorising it under member resources (MR), but he steers clear from the mention of psychological notions in his approach. However, van Dijk makes extensive use of social cognition in understanding discourse and interaction. Moreover, emerging trends in CDA highlight a marriage between cognition and language such as critical metaphor studies (Koller 2004; Charteris-Black 2011), cognitive language approach (Hart 2008, 2010) and proximation theory (Cap 2014). Mostly, these approaches focus on the use of "broader cognitive systems" (Hart and Cap 2014: 6) such as metaphors, conceptualisation, construal and proximation that bring into focus the ideological import of language.

Context and discourse

Teun A. van Dijk's sociocognitive approach to discourse is one of the most influential models that delve into the connections between language use and society from a psychological perspective. His approach is part of critical discourse studies that attempts to uncover the opaqueness and misrepresentation in language to study power relations and ideological beliefs in society. However, unlike the other critical approaches (Fairclough 1989; Wodak 1991), van Dijk assumes that the link between discourse and society is mediated through a cognitive or human interface whereby he proposes a detailed study of context to understand what is

18 Sociocognitive approaches

happening at multiple levels: sociocultural, psychological, historical, linguistic, etc. Context models as they are known are based on the reciprocal assumption that context and language influence each other (particularly the influence of context on language), and therefore contextualisation is fundamental to the understanding of human behaviour: "*con-texts* are called that way because etymologically they come *with* texts" (2008a: 5, emphasis original) and help describe a text in better ways. Thus, an elaboration of context in text and talk is part of his work. Context models are fundamental to the understanding of power dynamics and ideological beliefs that will be discussed later. In the social sciences, context is designated by different words such as situation, background and environment, prefixed by the name of the discipline in which it is being studied, like historical background or geographical environment (van Dijk 2008a). In linguistics, particularly discourse analysis, context is considered relevant only if it highlights some aspect of language use since the focus is on the latter. Some practitioners in conversation analysis even advocate a strict attention to interactional features (see Sacks, Schegloff and Jefferson 1974) while others use the notion of context to clarify what and how people use language (see Grice 1975; Brown and Levinson 1987). Therefore, hardly any theory of discourse analysis provide a mechanics for the description of context except Hymes's ethnography through its analysis of the speech patterns and components of the SPEAKING model *in situ*.

Without an analysis of context, language analysis can become stilted and artificial. For instance, a conversation between two persons on music can be better analysed not just by using discourse tools but by paying attention to the music they are speaking about, their gender, social status and other indices, all of which form a part of the larger context. In the words of van Dijk, "contexts are thus not some kind of objective condition or direct cause, but rather (inter) subjective constructs designed and ongoingly updated in interaction by participants as members of groups and communities" (2008a: x). This definition requires some understanding. Firstly, contexts are a subjective construction of what is happening depending on the speaker's perception, beliefs, emotions and attitudes. Contexts can be viewed as experiences that are "embedded in a set of autobiographical representations in episodic memory" (van Dijk, 2009: 249). A newspaper report on an earthquake would evoke diverse responses from two people, in fact even from the same person at different points of time. Secondly, these experiences are constantly updated in talk in daily experiences. Our knowledge about earthquakes, their intensity, preventive measure, etc., is updated as part of general conversation or through reading and writing. This means contexts are dynamic or ever changing, and they involve production or comprehension of that already spoken plus the new information in talk. How individuals process and understand information, and articulate their views, requires knowledge of what is known in discourse studies as the 'discourse record' – tailoring one's speech to what has already been said. In talking about natural calamities, one needs to comprehend what has been spoken in a conversation and then say something new to avoid repetition. Similarly, a news report about a novel disaster management measure adopted by the government can change the way in which scientists understand and talk about tackling natural calamities, for this information is now added to their existing repertoire of current affairs.

Context models

Context models are also known as mental models referring to the subjective experiences of participants about situations that are stored in one's memory and are made up of one's evaluative opinions, attitudes and feelings (van Dijk 2008a, 2009). The 'mental' aspect is a gamut of psychological processes that act as the interface for experiencing a situation and comprehending it, and this interface is not studied by discourse analysts, though it is a crucial component for understanding the multi-layeredness of human interaction, providing penetrating insights about human behaviour and personality. Unlike linguists who give primacy to language, the sociocognitive theorist analyses the human psyche as reflected through language use; language analysis is not the end but the means to an end. Another name for contexts is 'experience models' as they explore the subjective histories and perceptions of individuals about communicative situations. They "*are* our experiences if we assume experiences to be personal interpretations of what happens to us" (van Dijk, 2008a: 61) and that is why they include facts and opinions as cognitive representations. Since these experiences are unique to each person, their language and responses about a person or event can vary distinctly. For example, one's conversation on astronomy can be influenced by many factors, such as the setting, timing and the person one is speaking to, be it a family member, a colleague, a neighbour, a child, etc.

This aspect of the context model echoes the fundamental property of creativity and originality of language construction. Due to the variability of language use, therefore, context models provide a description for the pragmatics of discourse among the social actors. The above point is telling. Pragmatics is the study of meaning in context, and the way in which individuals speak or write indicates, firstly, that they have to be appropriate to the context, and secondly, that multiple meanings may arise from one's discourse, and hence it may have diverse interpretations. They have to employ the right kind of speech acts, politeness strategies, conversational implicature, deictic expressions to participate in all types of communication. Attention to discourse and its pragmatic meanings, then, is not a structural analysis of language but reveals the competence and appropriacy of interaction, and social practices and beliefs at large. This appropriateness can be found at many levels: "intonation, lexical selection, syntax, indexical expressions, topics, speech acts, turn distribution and so on" (van Dijk, 2008a: 21). So, how something is said is as important as what is said. The intended and the interpreted meanings highlight how things are represented and constructed in society and how individuals understand the world around them. In my view, this aspect of varied interpretation of discourse among speakers can be useful in critical discourse studies to contrast and compare the analyst's view with that of

20 Sociocognitive approaches

the respondents, bridging the gap between critical analysis and reception studies, a view echoed by others in advocating the triangulation approach (Weiss and Wodak 2003). Like other CDA theorists, van Dijk too conceives discourse as social action. Through talk, individuals don't just share information but negotiate meanings and their identities. They narrate their subjectivities and focus on each other, articulating their personal views and shared knowledge. Discourse, in other words, is intersubjective.

The dimensions of ideological meaning, power dynamics and social knowledge come to the fore, linking the personal to the social. The traditional Marxist view of ideology as false consciousness has been replaced by ideology as interpellation (Althusser 1971), whereby individuals are made into subjects and ideology functions through consent of the ideological state apparatuses such as the family, school, media, and religion. In discourse, ideology is understood as commonsensical notions articulated through discourse that serve and maintain the power structures in society. Therefore, intersubjectivity in talk allows each participant to fully comprehend the discourse of the other, respond accordingly and, in the process, air one's views which may be ideological, evaluative or normative. Since contexts are socially based (shared cognition, grammars, value–systems and norms), talk and text contain information about sociocultural views and practices, producing social knowledge about how things function in a particular society. Linguistic, cognitive and communicative resources help in the production and reproduction of such information. Thus, intersubjectivity, social knowledge and ideology are linked in complex but fascinating ways. For instance, conversation among two officer-goers about the practice of dowry among the Tamil Brahmins in Chennai is based on their intersubjective understanding of the concept, revealing their personal views and experiences along with the social norms and values which they might support, oppose or be neutral to.

Contexts are culturally variable, emphasising culture specific norms and appropriateness conditions for discourse, in different societies. Though some features can be universal, many others are specific, such as kinship terms, power and status that reveal the peculiarities of each culture. In the Indian context, kinship terms vary greatly from that of the Americans in number and names. The American term 'uncle' is a non-specific equivalent of Indian terms *chacha*, *mama*, *phoopha*, etc., depending on whether the uncle is from the paternal or maternal side. Such seemingly simple details are relevant for understanding how politeness, deference and interactional norms vary among cultures, in turn affecting what people can speak and how they can do so. The realisation of speech acts, particularly apologies and requests, among speakers from different communities has given rise to the domain of intercultural pragmatics (Blum-Kulka and Olshtain 1984). Similarly, cultural differences exist in the formal codified speech of Japanese and the relatively less formal talk of Americans and Spaniards (Hogg and Vaughan 2018).

Another aspect of contexts is that they are more or less planned, and this is because specific contexts develop from culturally shared knowledge, schemas, social categories and communicative acts; that is, local contexts are embedded in larger ones, reflecting broader cultural trends and norms. In fact, one can learn 'context types' as specific social situations and what can be said in them. What and how to speak at the counter for railway booking is different from a marriage event, each having its own context and language. Individuals can have shared memories about events and activities that aid in talking about them. Conversations about the Cricket World Cup matches are planned in the sense that one knows who is being talked about, the players, the matches, the fees, the past achievements and so on. However, not all communication is planned. Spontaneous interaction is also possible depending on what happens in the present context (say, the present cricket match) and the subjective reactions of the speakers. This clarifies two further properties of contexts, namely that they include relevant ongoing information and that they link micro- to macro-contexts. The micro-level analysis of language can insightfully point towards social trends and global happenings since each instance of language use is symbolic of bigger issues. Language not only shows what is happening but also has the power to change. It is this particular feature of van Dijk's model that makes it 'glocal,' addressing individual and group concerns, avoiding positivism and determinism in perspective. Also, such a theory presupposes that subjective description of communicative situations represents how people represent meaning and understand everyday experience through cognition to make the mundane more significant.

The notion of genres (Bhatia 1993) is also crucial in context models. A genre can be understood as a kind of written or spoken activity with similar features or properties such as riddles, debates, poetry, television news, storytelling or narration, arguments, etc. Van Dijk (2008a) differentiates between discourse genres that are characterised by specific linguistic or discourse features and context genres that are defined by the physical and temporal setting, the participants involved and their respective roles, the activities engaged in, their social cognition, the social or institutional domain, the mode of communication, etc. For instance, news debates on television air at a specific time, featuring a news anchor and guests who are involved in the roles of speaking for or against a topic. Similar is the case with business meetings, everyday talk, police interrogations, etc. The understanding of what happens in such a genre is based on actions, social practices or activity types. In contrast, discourse genres, or discourse structure types as van Dijk calls them (2008a), are characterised by discourse structures – such as the speech acts and politeness strategies, the turn-taking mechanism, lexis and argument structure, and rhetorical strategies. These are textual features that can occur across contexts. A news debate is characterised by frequent interruptions and uneven turns among the participants, cross-questioning and counter-arguments and debate openings and closings. A similar discourse structure can be found in parliamentary deliberations or classroom discussion. However, these two types of genres are not watertight categories but, in fact, they overlap, for textual properties can be similar across contexts. The moot difference is that context genres are defined by people and activity, whereas discourse genres by

22 Sociocognitive approaches

textual properties and every genre is defined in terms of both, depending on the relative importance given to structure or activity.

Context and social cognition

Context models are not synonymous with text and talk; therefore, what is the relationship between the two? In common parlance, text and talk constitute discourse while context is the environment for that discourse. Contexts create the base for text and talk and are largely implicit. Talk is indirectly influenced by context, and this becomes apparent in cases of misunderstanding or errors. Van Dijk reserves the term "communicative or interactional episode" (2008a: 25) for a combination of the two that are distinct from each other, even though discourse can be part of a larger context. This point shows a conceptual difference between this approach and that of others in social psychology who claim that discourse and context are the same (Edwards and Potter 1992). He asserts that discourse and context are related and shape each other but his model focusses on discursive action through a contextual understanding, particularly discourse representations of one's cognition in specific contexts. This can be explained by the following remark:

> *the definition, interpretation, representation or construction of participants* of their social situation, in terms of subjective context models, influences how they speak, write, read, listen and understand. In other words, societal or situational structures can only affect discourse through the mediation or the interface of the mental representations of language users.
>
> *(van Dijk, 2008a: 119, emphasis original)*

The context and its properties are inferred or indexed by the participants whenever necessary; however, it is not always spelt out in clear terms. For example, the talk on cricket is based on knowledge of cricket matches and players, and the speakers need not explicitly state that they are now going to talk about this topic and about male players! As and when they talk, topics and subtopics emerge, becoming a part of the interaction, even from the past, denoting that past contexts can influence present ones, much like intertextual links (Bakhtin 1994). A text refers to its previous texts (discursive aspect) as part of context in social settings (media, academic, bureaucratic, etc.) like referring to what someone else said, and an issue in contextual analysis is deciding how much of the previous contexts should be a part of the present analysis.

Since cognition links discourse to society, one of the central components of cognition is schema. Schemas (Bartlett 1932) are mental structures for organising the world around us (Baron 2001). Our everyday routine experiences, regarding meeting people or knowing about an event, are organised in set ways, so much so that the mere mention of an event or individual evokes knowledge about that category. For instance, an event like an Indian wedding includes generalisations

Sociocognitive approaches **23**

about a series of functions beginning with the *haldi* ceremony (applying turmeric paste to would-be bride and groom), the *sangeet* (dancing), the engagement and, later, the main rituals of marriage. Or one's dining experience in a restaurant presupposes seating at a table, selection of dishes from the menu, eating and payment of the bill. Schemas about events are known as scripts (Schank and Abelson 1977) and those about individuals are known as person schemas. Participants presuppose large amounts of social knowledge on their part which can be updated or activated when encountering a person or event category, and such information is implicitly brought by the participants in conversation for comprehension and production. In van Dijk's view, it makes sense to thus talk of context model as schema model – socially shared experiences having limited but fixed categories or 'contents' as follows:

1   Setting includes the time and physical setting of an event/activity described by various names as place, space and environment.
2   Participant framework consists of oneself and other(s) and can be subdivided into various relationships:

   a)   Communicative roles like speaker, hearer, addressor, addressee, reader, writer, messenger, relayer, etc. (for a detailed discussion, see Hymes 1972).
   b)   Social role types comprising social membership and identity that can be described in terms of professional, personal, national, religious or community-based roles.
   c)   Other relations between participants include social indices of gender, power, ideology, sexual orientation, caste and so on.

3   Socially shared knowledge and beliefs.
4   Intentions and goals.
5   Communicative events and other actions.

The personal experiences of participants in conversation are characterised by the central category of a Self that is egocentric, that tells them about where they are (spatiotemporal setting), who they are, what they are doing (speaking or writing) and with/to whom (the audience/hearers). The Self roughly corresponds to their identity that is known by various names such as subjectivity, self-representation, embodied-ness, self-awareness, etc. The Self is not a single, whole identity but is made up of multiple selves, such as your name, nationality, profession, relation with others in the family and so on, each of which puts you in different social roles. You can be a son, chef, footballer and Christian with left-wing political views. Thus, in one way, one's Self consists of several social roles that change through interaction and activities, based as they are on the evaluations and perceptions of other. In fact, psychological counselling informs us that there are many selves, based on not just one's perception and that of others but also what one aspires to be (Rogers 1951, 1957). Therefore, the Self is a composite term for the many versions of oneself that change throughout life; yet there seems to

24 Sociocognitive approaches

be some stability in one's core beliefs, values and identity, prompting van Dijk (2008a, 2009) to state that Self is also a stable concept, giving rise to self-schemas (Markus 1977), that is, what we think as our identity. Everyday interaction continuously updates one's notion of Self, making it a communicative accomplishment. For example, the notion of 'you' is in contrast to 'I,' and deictic verbs 'come' and 'go' are spoken with reference to the speaker's place of orientation (Levinson 1983; Cruse 2000): come here, go to the library. In discourse studies, the Self is central to discursive action, conversation and narration (van Dijk 2009) because it creates in-groups and out-groups on the basis of what one identifies with in contrast to others. For example, I can be a doctor and a member of the medical fraternity (in-group) in comparison to someone who is not (out-group). In addition, the Self in discourse is the experiencer and the recorder of one's life and history, and many researchers (Smith 1993) give primacy to accounts of the Self as authentic and credible voices.

Of particular importance is the conception of social cognition that has a strong basis in social psychology (van Dijk 1998, 2009). The context model includes a wide range of psychological phenomena under this category – beliefs, norms, attitudes, emotions and values – to study intergroup relations. A person can hold beliefs that can be evaluative and ideological if they perpetuate certain power relations in society; however, all beliefs are not ideological. Particular settings and people can evoke different emotions and feelings in a person, and one can say that one's attitude is a conglomerate of beliefs, feelings, norms and values. The strength of the approach lies in the fact that the operations of power and ideology can be seen through the psychological lens. Thus, what we say and write is clearly related to how we think and feel at the individual and group levels. In fact, the processes of persuasion, impression management and conformity are also examined as discursive strategies of how groups/individuals influence each other to achieve particular goals in social interaction.

Power and ideology

The analysis of power and ideology are crucial in critical discourse studies (CDS), with most approaches seeking to investigate power asymmetry, often through the ideological assumptions, beliefs and points of view of the participants involved in talk. Power is construed in different ways in CDS. Fairclough's (1992) analysis largely relies on the Foucauldian conception of power, whereas Wodak (1991) prefers a discursive-historical analysis to examine the issue of abuse of power. In his approach, van Dijk conceives of power and domination as "a specific relationship of control between social groups or organizations – and not as a property of interpersonal relations" (van Dijk, 2016: 71). Power is understood not only through language but material resources and symbolic means such as knowledge, high status, wealth, occupation, fame, skin colour, nationality and origin. Control is exercised over the actions and social cognition of the members of a community by the dominant groups and discourses are the main link through which the minds of people are regulated. Power has various forms: domination, struggle, manipulation etc. Manipulation, particularly, shows the effects of persuasion and the power of the speaker, and it involves the following strategies: emphasising the position of one's power and the lack of knowledge of the recipient, focussing on arguments and beliefs that the manipulator wants the audience to accept, discrediting opposing views and reasoning and appealing to the attitudes and ideologies of the listeners (van Dijk 2006). In an analysis of former British Prime Minister Tony Blair's speech in the House of Commons, van Dijk finds the use of the above-mentioned strategies wherein Blair engages in positive self-presentation, blaming the opposition (the Liberal Democrats) as opportunistic, presenting a polarisation between democracy (characterised as Good) versus dictatorship (symbolically Evil) as a means to go to war, all the while suggesting that the British Parliament has the right to decide to go to war (van Dijk 2006).

Ideologies, in contrast, are broadly defined as "socio-political cognitions of groups" (van Dijk, 1995: 138). Ideologies are not conceived in the Marxist sense as false consciousness that distort reality but as those evaluative beliefs and opinions that are in the service of power. Ideologies are normative beliefs that have become naturalised over a period of time and are shared by specific social groups. Legitimation of the dominant ideologies and control of resources is a form of manipulative power. Social cognition reflects the ideological beliefs of people in their interaction, and that is why context models are important for ideological analysis. Van Dijk (1995, 1998) discusses some of the essential ideological discourse structures that can be helpful in many kinds of analysis.

1 Identity/membership – polarisation between a positive representation of in-groups and negative representation of out-groups. For example, in racist discourse, the Whites evaluate themselves in favourable terms while judging minority communities (Hispanics, African-Americans) unfavourably. Pronouns are often used to serve polarisation creating two categories – Us and Them. Identification is another common process among members of ideological groups who identify with their groups. For example, 'I am a scientist' or 'I am a Hindu.'
2 Social position – emphasis of positive self-description that includes self-glorification or self-praise, simultaneously condemning the other as is commonly found in xenophobic discourses. The opposite rarely happens.
3 Activities – ideological groups engage in typical activities like attacking, criticising, maligning and controlling the out-group, and justifying their actions to do so.
4 Norms and values – evaluative statements by people directly and indirectly express their norms of conduct and values that in-groups strive to uphold such as freedom, equality, independence and justice.
5 Goals – ideological discourses are geared to protect the interests of the in-group, both material (food, place of living, jobs) and symbolic (status, access to public discourse).

26 Sociocognitive approaches

The text and talk (discourse) of people are studied as part of context models to understand the abuse of power and how the dominant groups act in their own interests against the benefit of the less powerful social groups. The variation in contexts, their culture specificity, the roles of participants, their use of language and the social beliefs encoded in their talk – all highlight individual and group ideologies, and the operationalisation of power. The analysis of newspaper articles on the terrorist bombing of the World Trade Center buildings in New York reveal the glaring polarisation between Americans and the rest of the world, especially Muslims, through the negative other-descriptions of the latter, the use of pronouns, self-glorification and negative lexicalisation among other strategies. For instance, the activities of the Other were described in forceful terms such as "paralyzing fear, inflaming hatred, gangs, murky, poisoned, obsession" (van Dijk, 1995: 154). In his analysis, van Dijk found "blatant nationalism and ethno-centrism" (1995: 150) and one possible reason could be that most of the opinion articles were written by American nationals.

Discursive features

Discourse in van Dijk's approach has developed from a semantic and pragmatic account to the employment of mental models. Initially, discourse was conceived in terms of semantic and global coherence, a functional relation between propositions at the micro-level in a text and macrostructures at the social level. However, the full meaning of a text could not be accounted for at the textual level; therefore, the cognitive dimension (mental models or context models) was formulated to underline the link between the discursive, the personal and the social. With the introduction of new theories and concepts in discourse (see Chapter 1 for a discussion), van Dijk's approach takes a very exhaustive view of discourse including the following features (van Dijk 2008a, 2009) in its analysis (due to space constraints, the features are mentioned, not described):

1   Genres and styles of speaking and writing.
2   Principles of turn-taking mechanism such as sequential patterns, topics, interruptions, silences and talk organisation.
3   Argumentation strategies and genres.
4   Rhetorical strategies for persuasion and control.
5   Deixis and presuppositions.
6   Speech acts and implicature.
7   Politeness strategies.
8   Lexical selection including figurative language such as metaphors.
9   Narrative structure including introduction/orientation, complication, interesting events, resolutions, commentary and conclusions/coda.

The obvious advantage of such a range of concepts is the flexibility it lends to the analysis because discourse features are text specific and not all are applicable to each text. Drama, for instance, would make greater use of turn-taking mechanism, while lexis, speech acts and argumentation strategies might be more suitable for news reports. Discourse analysis of news reports and racist discourse was in fact carried out by van Dijk; thus, a word about each is given next.

News discourse

The study of news discourse and its broad areas (news structure, production and comprehension) by van Dijk (1988) was novel in its approach because of the following reasons. Primarily it laid emphasis on the psychological, social and the linguistic aspects of news production, arguing that news production was not a simple, linear process but a complex machinery that involved reporters to editors that took decisions on reporting, monitoring and broadcasting. Moreover, this kind of investigation emphasised social knowledge, schemas and the role of memory in interpersonal communication, even though the theory of context models was not fully developed in those times. However, van Dijk proposed that reports were arranged according to news schema that inform about the action, time, setting, participants, etc. I think that the elaboration of the following news schema categories hold theoretical and practical relevance, indicating what to 'see' when doing analysis:

1   Summary – headlines and lead are in bold font and express the main topic.
2   Episode – this includes the main event and its background.
3   Consequences of the episode(s) that indicate the newsworthiness of a news item and give "causal coherence" (van Dijk, 1988: 54) to the entire topic.
4   Verbal reactions that create 'objective' opinions by the use of 'sources,' quotes, names of witnesses, etc.
5   The heading comment comprises the evaluation of and expectations about the news events.
6   Ordering of news categories, top-down, is according to the principle of relevance

At the local or micro-level, a news text can be analysed according to the following features:

1   Local semantics and propositions that show the clause complexity and structure.
2   Local coherence highlighted through relations of conditional clauses, cause-effect links, temporal adverbs and factuality.
3   Topics and knowledge are understood through schemas, scripts, presuppositions, beliefs, opinions and ideologies.
4   Word order and news style aims to be impersonal, formal, objective since news is public discourse.

28 Sociocognitive approaches

5   Rhetorical strategies such as emphasis on fact, quoting 'reliable sources,' arousing sensationalism, strong emotions and ideological leanings indicate the truthfulness of events.
6   The cognitive or attitudinal elements show that it increases the "effectiveness of news" (van Dijk, 1988: 83) and involves complex argumentation.

In comparison to the useful guidelines for analysing news, van Dijk's study of news comprehension highlighted the psychological effects of media. He selected four news items from two main Dutch dailies and interviewed people in three stages – an initial free recall interview, a delayed recall interview after two weeks and a control experiment in laboratory conditions, all using the same material. The participants were asked what they read on a particular day and to describe in their own words what they had read. The study was an important contribution because it demonstrated that the discourse of news structure was clearly linked to its recall value, since most participants remembered the main news even though they claimed to remember more. Also, the powerful influence of media was highlighted since many media forms (radio, television) interfered with the recalling of news items in everyday life. Moreover, the phenomenon of self-deception was clearly visible, since participants recalled only one-third of the news but claimed to remember more.

Racist discourse

Other studies by van Dijk (1984, 1988) deal with the ubiquity of racism across public domains (corporate sector, politics, academics and education) through informal interviews (more than a hundred) conducted with the Dutch. Their significance can be understood through the common yet insightful findings at the everyday level. Majority-group members typically present themselves in a favourable light so that they are accepted and respected, and their views about the minority community are organised around an ethnic attitude schema that is both personal and socially shared. Talk about minorities is stereotypical regarding the topics that are discussed, such as crime, violence, work, housing and social benefits, and the stories about them focus on how they are a nuisance (negative other presentation) and how nothing can be done against them due to their adverse traits of aggression, laziness, demanding nature, backwardness, etc. Polarisation into Us-Them is common, as are lack of a resolution category (not stating the reasons for the minorities' condition) and the presence of an evaluative category that delves on the negative opinions of the majority community's members. Conversation about minorities also begins with self-defence or such justification as 'I have nothing against them but . . .' and along with the above argumentation strategies, it lends social credence to the undertakings of the majority. If derisive talk about the ethnic communities transpires, it is consciously stopped or rephrased in accordance with the norms of political correctness. The study attempts to explain the sociocognitive effect of such routine conversation, harping at the pervasiveness of prejudice.

In fact, van Dijk (1984, 1988, 2008b) explores the ramifications of prejudice across domains, indicating its ubiquity at social, educational and political spheres of life. An examination of parliamentary deliberations in American and European countries shows the argumentation strategies used by parliamentarians to talk about minorities. Often, the lexis of natural calamities like 'deluge,' 'earthquake' and 'flood' are used to talk about their influx. Other strategies include recourse to popular opinion, justification that political measures against the minority community are taken for their own good and emphasis on their negative traits despite the majority community's attempts to help them. In the corporate sector, too, ambivalence can be noticed in their attempts to maintain a fair, non-racial image and standard arguments such as 'we are not a welfare organisation' or 'we select the best candidate' are put forth justifying the non-inclusion of others. Talk on discrimination is often met with self-defence and face-keeping arguments, presenting oneself positively and the ethnic group negatively, and storytelling is used as a persuasive strategy to support one's viewpoints. Even in educational discourse, the examination of textbooks on sociology show that many of them present information neutrally, maintaining the status quo about racism in America and Europe, and not focussing too much on the wider implications of discrimination at the personal, social and everyday levels.

Metaphor: a critical cognitive perspective

The work by Veronika Koller (2004) falls under the broad domain of critical cognitive studies that examines metaphors in business media discourse, both quantitatively and qualitatively. The study of metaphor has a long history in other areas before being properly addressed as part of discourse analysis. Metaphor has long been considered a figurative device in literary discourse (Childs and Fowler 2006), and it has been studied by cognitive linguists and psychologists as well (Lakoff and Johnson 1980; Gibbs 1994; Fauconnier and Turner 2002). However, discourse analysts contend that it is very much a part of language studies, its ideological effects are far reaching and it is a powerful indicator of social and political changes (Chilton 1987; Hart 2008). In fact, critical discourse analysts advocate an examination of metaphors as part of a critical analysis of language (Fairclough 1989; van Dijk 2006). Before we discuss Koller's research, a word about the earlier, seminal cognitive research is relevant. The conceptual metaphor theory (Lakoff and Johnson 1980) analyses conventional metaphors and metonymy in terms of a mapping process between two domains – target and source – and through their penetrating analysis, they propose that the use of metaphors is ubiquitous, systematic, unconscious and unidirectional, whereby the target domain predominates in the social and cultural spheres of human existence. Metaphors are part of a broad conceptual system that is deeply entrenched in the human psyche, and an analysis of metaphors often includes sub-categories

30 Sociocognitive approaches

that can point at the ways in which our culture and thinking is organised. For example, 'time as money' might include the sub-metaphors of time as a limited resource and time as a valuable commodity:

> You're *wasting* my time.
> I don't *have* the time to *give* you.
> I don't *have enough* time to *spare* for that. You're *running out* of time.
> He's living on *borrowed* time.
>
> *(Lakoff and Johnson, 1980: 8–9,*
> *emphasis original)*

An outstanding contribution of the study was its cognitive basis for language; that metaphors provide a coherent structuring for human experience because abstract notions (like love and jealousy) are incomplete without metaphorical understanding. Lakoff and Johnson explained in detail metaphoric mappings (source to target domains), and also how schemas, prototypes, frames and metonymy functioned through metaphorical structuring. Their approach was seminal in underscoring the pervasiveness and deep-rootedness of metaphors in human thought and how systematic and stable metaphor mappings were; but they did not discuss how conceptual integration occurred, how old ideas could be creatively paired with new to frame new ideas.

Blending theory (Fauconnier and Turner 2002) takes metaphor mapping for granted and instead focusses on conceptual integration, that is, how conceptual spaces (words, ideas and images) are combined for use in imaginative and novel cases to re-understand the identity of something, its likeness and difference. The theorists use the example of skiing to explain conceptual integration. The ski instructor asks the learner to "pretend that we are 'pushing off' by roller skating" (2002: 21); however, one cannot think of pushing off on roller skates, as they might fall down and hurt themselves badly, therefore one has to "selectively combine the action of pushing off with the action of skiing" producing a blend, a "new emergent pattern" called skating (Ibid.). Blending processes are also indicators of our social and psychological surroundings, and they are ubiquitous. However, they are multi-dimensional wherein the inferencing occurs from the blend to the target, helping to understand old ideas in new ways. Thus, the theory successfully showed the cognitive functioning and patterning done by the brain to build new connections and understand the environment. Although both approaches had a strong cognitive basis and explained how cognition worked through language, they did not explore how metaphoric mapping operated in discourse. Moreover, the critical angle to the use of metaphors in everyday life was not accounted for.

In contrast to these earlier approaches, Koller proposes a novel way for investigating metaphors that kindled her interest while studying "the perceived dominance of the WAR metaphor in business media discourse" (2004: 3). Since CDA does not pay detailed attention to metaphor study, her contention is that it is relevant to focus on the "sociocultural and ideological functions of metaphor"

Sociocognitive approaches **31**

(2004: 8), since people can hide behind the use of metaphors and absolve themselves from being held responsible for their speech. Her approach is discursive and psychological in the sense that it assumes that discourse participants "draw on a pool of complex metaphors" to understand and negotiate "social identities and relations through text" (2004: 9). In short, the strength of Koller's approach lies in how individuals use and understand metaphors, socially and cognitively, in discourse. Thus, in one stroke she links discourse, psychology and critical theory.

Koller argues that primary metaphors are blended into complex metaphors through various processes of clustering and hybridisation, and everyone has a pool of such metaphors and its expressions for understanding everyday life. Access to the pool is determined by an interplay of social and personal cognitive factors. Social cognition, as we know from van Dijk's model (2006), influences and is influenced by discursive factors and, therefore, metaphor use is a part of discourse production. By constructing the world in metaphorical terms, the writers create particular kinds of discourses that structure the reader's world in specific cognitive ways. For instance, arguments are viewed as war with opponents requiring strategising and planning on how to attack and defend (Lakoff and Johnson 1980). Metaphors determine text production and comprehension and are, therefore, capable of manifesting ideology, hegemonic relations in society, challenging or transforming them or perpetuating the status quo. This is a cyclical process where metaphors are used and comprehended through the matrix of discourse, cognition and ideology. In fact, Koller states that, "social cognition is at work at every stage after the formation of primary metaphors" (2004: 42).

Koller's empirical research included investigating a large corpus of newspapers plus magazine articles about marketing and sales, and mergers and acquisitions (M&A), combining computer-assisted quantitative analysis with qualitative analysis using Halliday's functional grammar. Clusters (frequent co-occurrence) of dominant metaphors were analysed, and it was found that in the case of sales and marketing the main metaphor clusters were war, sports and games, while in the case of M&A it was more of an evolutionary struggle that included the domains of fighting, feeding, mating and occasionally dancing that served as an alternative metaphor. Most of the words were grammatically nouns in the case of fighting and mating metaphors. One of the reasons for the use of war metaphors (like campaign, launch and target) in marketing is gender – war is associated with the discourses of hegemonic masculinity, aggression and leadership, effacing feminine qualities, making marketing a male-dominated area. The subsequent rankings were that of the sports and games metaphors, and in each case, a correspondence could be seen in terms of the lexical items used in discourse. War metaphors were noun-heavy, while sports metaphors used more verbs. Koller also argues that as an ideological discursive practice, writers should use alternative metaphors to avoid stereotyping and reification of the social order. In another study, Koller (2005) investigated the dominant verbal metaphors in marketing and M&A and their corresponding visual metaphoric designs, finding a high correlation between the two. Magazines supported their writing with

32 Sociocognitive approaches

visual illustrations of the same material, and most metaphors belonged to the war/fighting domain, creating a single gestalt that was predominant in business media discourse. A related study employed qualitative and quantitative means (Demmen et al. 2015) to highlight the excessive use of metaphors of violence, particularly military metaphors, for cancer patients who were about to end their lives, by the patients themselves, their caretakers and health professionals. Their use of metaphorical language to talk about the adversarial perception of how they were being treated medically has serious implications for healthcare and communication studies.

In the case of M&A, there exists the metaphor of takeovers as rapes, yet it is conspicuous by its absence because of the brutal connotations of the word. Rape is a cultural taboo, and in its place the mating metaphor is more common because it is easier to write about sexual violence against women under this category, sustaining the patriarchal mindset. In the mating metaphor, the acquired companies are seen as 'female' and 'weak,' while the fighting metaphors glorify masculinity and aggression. Koller's main premise is that masculinity is a valued social practice in business organisations (due to the preponderance of masculinised metaphors), and this is precisely the reason why there is need for change in their usage. The ideological effects of masculinity need to be rewritten to allow a re-viewing of the social order. The fact that the writers and the readers are mostly men is problematic itself, for it shows a skewed gendered readership, and such metaphors therefore make it easier to accept and condone actions that can otherwise be considered ethically problematic. One of the promising suggestions is that since metaphors are neurally wired, they can also be changed, creating hope for a more gender-neutral worldview. Koller's study, unlike the earlier ones, does not restrict itself to a mere cognitive examination of metaphors but provides a novel way of viewing metaphors as a psychological concept linked to discourse. The perception of gender through metaphors reinforces its widespread use and the social structuring of thought. Her approach gives voice to the complexity of thinking and therefore the spaces for transformational change. Unlike the earlier studies in CDA, it also combines qualitative and quantitative analysis for examining individual and social phenomena. However, the study does not incorporate reader reactions to metaphors, especially how they comprehend and process texts that contain metaphors, which is a crucial part of discourse reception and analysis.

In recent times, Koller (2014) has analysed collective identities combining critical discursive and sociocognitive approaches. Drawing on Moscovici (2000), she employs the concept of sociocognitive representations (CSRs) which are cognitive structures held by the members of a group about their goals, behaviour, values, emotions, expectations and attitudes that are manifested through discourse in interaction. These representations shape the way a group thinks and behaves in society and are therefore fundamental to the power relations and ideological clashes between groups. Koller is of the view that people make use

Sociocognitive approaches **33**

of CSRs in conversation in dealing with one another, and collective identity is therefore discursive and actional, constructed through the social and discursive practices that people engage in. Corresponding to Fairclough's three-stage approach (1989, 1992), she elaborates:

1   The micro-level of textual analysis that explores how collective identities are produced.
2   The meso-level of production, distribution, consumption and appropriation of discourses that examines people and their roles in discourse and the goals/functions of discourse.
3   The macro-level of social changes that looks at why collective identities are created the way they are.

The ways in which individuals evaluate group behaviour highlight the beliefs and expectations that each group has from the other, defining the way they are represented. Koller analyses a brief extract from an interview with a police officer, where an ideological clash occurs between the officer and the interviewer on the use of the phrase 'customer focus,' since both parties hold differing views regarding the behaviour of police. While the police officer's discourse is centred on how the police is providing services to the public with 'customer focus,' the interviewer objects to the use of this phrase, subscribing to the more traditional view of policemen as protectors and community helpers. Their views represent their conflicting CSRs, and since the work of the police has a direct impact on society and in today's times the audience is responsive through digital media platforms, the stakes are high for the conflict producers. This analysis demonstrates how ideological clashes are embedded in instances of language use, essentially being a discord between two belief systems represented by members of two groups.

Cognitive language approach

This approach, developed by Christopher Hart (2010, 2014), seeks to explore the "cognitive import of (ideologically imbued) linguistic representations" (Hart, 2014: 167). Like van Dijk's approach, this one, too, seeks to bridge the gap between language and cognition on the assumption that discourse and society are linked through cognition or the way we think and understand the world around us, and through repeated use cognitive structures become the basis for ideologies. In contrast to van Dijk's social psychology leanings, this approach has a basis in cognitive psychology. The cognitive linguistic approach (CLA) identifies four processes through which reality is represented.

Structural configuration occurs through schematisation that involves an abstract understanding of what a scene or event is, how something happens, its sequence, cause and the individual roles. Action schemas that denote the actions

34 Sociocognitive approaches

of actors and motion schemas that denote movement are common processes. For example, the following headline denotes action by the law makers:

> Muzzafarnagar riots: Non-bailable warrants issued against six accused in Kawal killing case
>
> *(Times of India headline, 14 February 2019)*

In essence, viewing a complex scene in terms of its parts helps to comprehend and simplify the complexity of it. The configuration can be expanded through other processes like framing, which involves understanding the qualities and attributes of individual aspects of a scene (the actors, actions and processes) in terms of categorisation and metaphors that carry specific connotations and associations. Framing occurs to compare, contrast and fully interpret domains of experience. In the above instance, the categories of riots, the victim and the accused become clear through the headline. In the example below, the headline metaphorises the cricket team from Rajasthan as underdogs and then negates it through the orientational metaphor of rising.

> Underdogs no more: the rise of Rajasthan and ilk
>
> *(Hindustan Times, 24 December 2011)*

Identification strategies, known through shifts in one's point of view, refer to the relative importance or absence of the social actors in the scene. The shifts can be compared to the zooming in and out of a camera to provide close-up or distant views of the scene and its actors. Positioning strategies, in contrast, refer to the use of metaphors (literal or figurative) in understanding the actors and events in the scene. It also involves the use of deictic markers and adverbs related to space and time to position a narrative or point of view. The fundamental argument in CLA is that the narrative can be understood through cognitive operations, since meaning-making is a cognitive activity. Our ideas about time, space and distance are construed cognitively, and therefore, CLA represents a bold attempt to understand the discursive through the psychological.

Yet another concept that is gaining currency in discourse studies is that of proximation which means to bring closer, and Cap (2006, 2014) uses it as a cognitive-linguistic process through which faraway/distant happenings or occurrences are made to appear closer and potentially threatening and hazardous to the speaker and the audience. This is one of the strategies used by the media to make war imminent and the enemy dangerous, and it is therefore a basic tool for legitimising particular actions and policies and unearthing their ideological currents.

Summing up

Since CDA theorists have largely ignored the workings of the mind, the emergence of sociocognitive approaches affords the analyst wider scope in analysing

Sociocognitive approaches **35**

cognitive representations of social phenomena, demonstrating that the use of language is related to how we think and feel. However, most approaches have focussed primarily on metaphors, except context models. Although CLA provides a wider discussion of cognitive concepts in comparison to Koller's exclusive focus on metaphors, Koller's work on metaphors of gender is no less significant since it demonstrates the organisation of social thought and practice. Also, Koller's and van Dijk's lucidity of language is in contrast to CLA's conceptually dense theorisation, although relevant. The two approaches on metaphor are not as wide in scope as context models; Koller, in fact, draws from it. Possible reasons could be that the latter explores cognition in social interaction through several tools and concepts, and through a cognitively alive human interface whose reactions and evaluations are dynamic and constantly updated. Thus, cognition and discourse are dynamic interfaces. The approach has a lot of scope in the areas of discourse and social psychology, for it provides a contextual understanding of people's subjectivities, connecting their personal beliefs to social norms and micro-contexts to macro- ones, through written and spoken discourses. However, the model does not explicitly discuss the issues of text reception (Breeze 2011), for the responses of people to a text are not simple and unproblematic; they can differ according to their attitudes and perceptions (van Dijk and Kintsch 1983), and they can highlight how people understand texts in media, politics, gender and other areas. Context models have wide applicability in gender and media studies to study culture-specific phenomena if combined with reception of texts (Sharma 2018).

Suggested reading

Wodak and Meyer's *Methods of Critical Discourse Studies* (2016) contains a lucid exposition of the approaches to CDA, including the sociocognitive approach. A more detailed description with analysis can be found in van Dijk's article on ideological discourse analysis (1995). Out of van Dijk's many publications, the ones on discourse and context (2008a) and an interdisciplinary approach to ideology (1998) are quite helpful for research. Koller's work on critical metaphor studies (2004) and Hart and Cap's edited volume on CDA (2014) can serve as useful guides for understanding emerging approaches in CDA.

3

DISCOURSE AND ACTION

Basic issues

Discursive psychology is an umbrella term for a conglomeration of approaches and perspectives in psychology that engage in qualitative analysis of talk and writing as social action, rather than a quantitative analysis of data using standardised procedures and tests. This chapter maps and evaluates the basic tenets of discursive psychology (DP), outlining the discursive action model (DAM) proposed by Edwards and Potter in their seminal work by the same name (1992). As the name implies, the aim of the approach is to study the link between cognition and reality by analysing how people:

> topicalize or orientate themselves to, or imply, in their discourse. And rather than seeing such discursive constructions as expressions of speakers' underlying cognitive states, they are examined in the context of their occurrence as situated and occasioned constructions whose precise nature makes sense, to participants and analysts alike, in terms of the social actions those descriptions accomplish.
>
> *(Edwards and Potter, 1992: 2–3)*

The above quotation points at a few significant features of the approach. Firstly, discourse is not viewed in linguistic or pragmatic terms in discursive psychology, as words, sentences, speech acts, politeness strategies that focus on the linguistic and meta-linguistic meanings created, but as constructions that are action-oriented. The meta-meanings generated are not analysed linguistically, but the interactional action itself is analysed. Therefore, discursive psychologists explore how people report, describe contrasting versions of the same event, attribute responsibility, claim accountability, remember events, show cause-effect link and how they draw inferences about people and events, assuming that people's speech is not objective. The examination is both of and for the event/ activity, including what the participants and witnesses speak, problematising the description as something to be solved and as something that includes its own explanation. For example, witness accounts of domestic violence are descriptions that can be examined as how and why someone witnessed such an act. Secondly, discourse is not seen as a reflection of one's mind and as expressing what is underlying, but mind and the social world/reality are "at issue in discourse" (Edwards, 1997: 20), locally produced and rhetorically expressed in descriptions of events and actions, mundane or technical. As Edwards and Potter state, "studying everyday discourse undermines the effort to apply laboratory findings to worldly practices, and encourages a reappraisal of the relations between language and cognition" (1992: 17). Therefore, this approach is against mentalism and in favour of 'epistemic' constructionism – how descriptions are constructed, not the larger social issues analysed through those descriptions (social constructionism). This is in contrast with the sociocognitive approaches, especially van Dijk's that links micro-analysis of talk to larger social issues and focusses on the critical perspective. In one sense, DP also explores culture, its practices and activities by becoming a part of them; that is, a discursive psychological interpretation of an event is reflexive, for it is just an interpretation among the many that may exist, an alternative version, so to say. In short, it is a cultural production like the culture it attempts to analyse. DP, therefore, views discourse and reality in two ways: as constructed through words, categories and other elements, and constructive in the sense that versions of reality are created and stabilised in interaction (Potter and Hepburn 2007). Often, discursive psychologists are accused of creating a new name for concepts that already exist in traditional psychology like impression management and self-presentation; however, Edwards and Potter (1992) claim that DP is radically different from the above two topics in the sense that they are interested in the discourses of the participant that creates an impression on the other and/or the discourses that speakers draw on to construct a positive self-image before others. Thus, their approach is theoretically and foundationally different from traditional psychologists since it presents a re-orientation of the social world and its practices (Wiggins 2017).

Discursive psychology and language

In an effort to understand DP's emphasis of language, one needs to examine how language was studied earlier. Earlier research in psychology viewed language in broadly two ways. One was the Chomskyan notion of linguistic competence (grammatical knowledge and organisation) and its study of an ideal, homogenous speaker-hearer environment, free from distractions, in contrast to actual speech punctuated with non-fluency markers that seemed disorderly and relatively unstructured. Chomsky (1959) upheld the psychological reality of linguistic structures and the biological working of the mind through the language acquisition device (LAD) that pre-programmed individuals to learn language – views

38 Discourse and action

commonly subsumed under the names of mentalism, cognitivism or nativism. Cognitivism reduced all language, psychological processes and talk to computational or mental processes, valuing the uniformity in decontextualised sentences, undermining the richness and complexity of natural talk. The other issue was an argument in favour of the pre-existence of cognitive processes, independent of language, as seen in the cognitive faculty of normal (Piaget 1952; Butterworth and Grover 1988; Leslie 1988) and differently abled children, animals, adults with language impairment, etc., understood through the retrospective linguistic readings of subjects' performances (Edwards 1997). A similar line of thinking is seen in cognitive semantics that (Lakoff and Johnson 1980; Wierzbicka 1992) advocate, the existence of cognition and language through decontextualised examples, and in computational science where the computer processes information like intelligent humans, accepting, manipulating, storing and recognising symbols (Neisser 1976). Criticising the conceptual metaphor theory (Lakoff and Johnson 1980), Edwards (1997) notes that language in DP is not viewed in terms of mental representation, deriving from bodily experience, giving primacy to such universalist cognitive phenomena but seen as public performance or performative discourse. There is little relevance in describing metaphors of love or anger across cultures ('I am crazy for you'/'She is mad at you') but to see how they are functionally used in talk to evoke multiple meanings. Similarly, DP does not agree with the deterministic view of language influencing thought, as found in the Whorf–Sapir Hypothesis. Categorisations of objects, events, humans such as table, chair, doctor, picnic, etc., are not mental but draw upon "*imagined social practices*" (Edwards, 1997: 259, emphasis original) and thus it is better to see how these categories are locally used to construct meanings as part of interaction, specific to a culture. Thus, overall, the reductionist cognitivist thinking that the external world is processed, understood and expressed in cognitive terms without recourse to social interaction is discarded in favour of descriptive talk as discursive action. Thus, DP is clearly anti-Cartesian and anti-cognitivist in perspective. A similar anti-mentalist stance is seen in the sociocognitive approach of van Dijk, who relies heavily on notions from social psychology. However, due to varying orientation, discursive psychology and context models focus differently on talk.

Major themes in discursive psychology

Since DP is primarily concerned with cognition, the latter is dealt in three ways in DP (Potter and Edwards 2003). Firstly, respecification and critique involves managing "psychological topics in terms of situated discourse practices" (Potter and Edwards, 2003: 170). While in social and cognitive psychology, topics such as attribution, memory and scripts are understood through experiments, DP reworks those topics as discourse practices (Edwards and Potter 1992, 1993; Edwards 2005). It analyses mostly interview talk by focussing on how people invoke psychological states when they are narrating events or describing reports.

Discourse and action **39**

Examples of this include how they use emotions in handling relationship disputes (Edwards 1999) or the use of scripts (Schank and Abelson 1977), better known as event schemas, in routine descriptions and what people do through those descriptions. A major assumption in DP is that psychological states such as attitudes, memory and script knowledge do not exist in people's minds but are formulated through one's actions and talk in the way they describe and claim accountability, presenting their versions of events. For example, in media reports, responsibility is avoided by the use of the term 'sources' or through witness accounts that give information. DP is interested in such a reconstruction in talk because it respecifies the event from the speaker's point of view, highlighting his actions. In another study on the construction of memory, Locke and Edwards (2003) highlight how memory can be used as a rhetorical resource to affirm or deny events and happenings, thereby saving oneself as happens in the case of Bill Clinton's interrogation by a grand jury regarding his relationship with Monica Lewinsky.

```
 8   I hav- (.) I hav – I know that Monica Lewinsky
 9   (0.6) came to the gate (.) on (.) the sixth,
10   (0.5) and uh (.) apparently directly (.) called
11   in and wanted to see me (.) and couldn't, (.)
12   and was angry about it.
```
(Locke and Edwards, 2003: 242)

Clinton shows problems in recalling the event, signalled by the use of repair mechanisms – I have – and the use of the word 'apparently' which shows that he cannot be held responsible for what he is saying since there are problems in memory recall. Nothing can be said with certainty, and in this manner he protects himself from claiming full responsibility of what he said. Later, when asked if Lewinsky was angry about the event, he responds in the affirmative, stating that he learnt about her anger from Betty (as quoted by the researchers), thus denying complete responsibility for his speech.

Secondly, psychological thesaurus deals with the management and description of common psychological states described as "the situated, occasioned, rhetorical uses of the commonsense lexicon of psychology. This involves a study of the practical use of terms such as *angry, jealous, believe, like, feel* and so on" (Potter and Edwards, 2003: 171, emphasis original). DP seeks to understand how people create versions of "their own thoughts, memories, feelings" when constructing versions of reality (Potter and Hepburn, 2007: 165). When one states 'I am angry' or 'I am jealous of you,' discursive psychologists are interested in what business is performed through such emotional statements as part of everyday, social or institutional interaction (Harré and Parrott 1996; Potter 1996; Edwards 1999). This belief in the use of everyday psychological terms in natural talk is in stark contrast to the emphasis on technical vocabulary in cognitive psychology that assumes such everyday talk to be messy and inaccurate (Edwards 2005). Moreover, emotional terms when used with cognitive verbs such as 'know' or 'believe'

40 Discourse and action

are useful in indicating who claims responsibility and how they do so in their descriptions. An example cited by Edwards (2005) is how the British newspaper the *Sun* responded to Princess Diana's brother, the Earl of Spencer, who said in an earlier interview how he firmly believed that the invasion of the media would lead to Diana's death and the *Sun* reported that he was liable to be 'bitter' in his grief but there was no need to put the blame on the press for her death. The Earl of Spencer's response, especially the use of 'always' and 'believe' show how his feelings of sadness are mixed with his judgement, and his emotional assessment is used by the press to prevent any attack on them, claiming that Spencer's response springs from grief. His bitterness, the press claims, is due to her death, not the paparazzi, absolving them of any responsibility. This example indicates how the use of emotions (such as worry, surprise, happiness, jealousy, anger, disgust) in talk is a means to justify oneself, accuse, counter-attack, question, or measure people's attitudes to an incident. Edwards (1997) argues for a move away from cognitive, etymological, semantic and conceptual understanding of emotions to emotion discourse, which is the functional use of emotions in everyday contexts through the multitudinous ways in which they can be talked of, to throw light on people's actions, indicate rational accountability or irrationality, individual dispositions, temporary actions, passive versus controlled behaviour, ethics, private versus public expression of thought, spontaneous versus externally caused behaviour and honest versus fake actions. Because of such variation in emotional display, situated talk can give a lot of insight about "flexible, accountability oriented, rhetorical work" (Edwards, 1997: 196). Discursive psychologists, thus, aim to explore not the metaphors for emotions and the perceptual-cognitive assumptions related to it, but the construction of emotional talk in everyday lives of people. Similarly, in sociocognitive approaches, emotions are subsumed under cognition and can be studied in discourse but, unlike this approach, not much emphasis is given to them. In the cognitive metaphor theories, too, emotions are viewed as the basis for the cognitive mapping of metaphors, not so much as a direct operation of emotions through discourse.

The phenomenon of intersubjectivity, whereby participants in talk assume mutual knowledge that acts as the basis for further interaction, can be studied discursively rather than in psycholinguistic terms. In cognitive terms, psychologists would attempt to pin the phenomenon to the mental states of people; but in DP, Edwards (2004) argues, it can be investigated through the sequential flow of conversation, using CA. Analysing a conversation between two persons (Lesley and Ed) about Ed's private teaching, the conversation veers to a boy whom Ed teaches, referred to as the "north Cadbury boy called Neville Cole" (Edwards, 2004: 46), and Lesley initially seems to acknowledge that she knows the boy but later denies it. When she denies knowing Neville Cole, Ed pursues the matter, speaking some more on the topic. However, Lesley cannot recognise the boy, stating that there are many boys with the same surname (Coles); but Ed gives more details about the boy, after which Lesley finally remembers and replies in the affirmative, even stating that she knows the boy and his family. This brief conversation has some pauses, which can indicate Ed's difficulty regarding the extent of Lesley's knowledge about Neville and how to make her remember the boy. Therefore, Ed provides more details, orienting himself and Lesley to the topic until she recalls and recognises Neville. Edwards, thus, argues that the question of what the participants don't know and how they get to know can be seen in interaction.

Thirdly, managing psychological implications refers to how DP studies psychological themes of anxiety, doubt, belief, prejudice and emotional investment as part of talk without those themes being overtly labelled. Here, one does not explicitly attribute blame or intent to someone by stating that they are doing so, but through seemingly straightforward and neutral descriptions of events and reportage of facts. In other words, 'fact and accountability' are the central themes explored in DP (Edwards and Potter 1992, 2001). Extreme Case Formulations (Pomerantz 1978, 1984) like 'the best,' 'the worst,' and 'the most' help to show how emotions and attitudes are configured in discourse and how people blame or attribute intention to others in actual talk. For example, Edwards (2005) reports the talk between two women, L and M, about L's mother-in-law Mrs. Field who has treated a person called Louisa very badly, and therefore she should not complain if she is not invited to Louisa's memorial service. The term used by M for her is 'so wicked,' an extreme case formulation that expresses L and M's extent of blame on Mrs. Field. Not just extreme case formulation, but other common expressions like 'to be honest,' 'quite frankly,' etc., are used discursively by the speakers in everyday talk. Since it is assumed that speakers are being relevant and honest in what they are saying (Grice 1975), the use of what Edwards and Fasulo (2006) call 'honesty phrases' can be interesting to study. Citing examples from various kinds of talk, the researchers are of the view that these phrases are used in case of dispreferred responses. This is a term used in CA to refer to responses made by the hearer that are not appropriate to the context; for instance, an offer requires an acceptance in most cases, and therefore, a refusal can be treated as a dispreferred response. When a speaker has to make a dispreferred response to a question, it might be considered insensitive, and his motive or attitude can be viewed negatively by the questioner; therefore, he tends to use 'honesty phrases' to mitigate the force of his response. In such situations, there is an implication that the speaker has to give an answer, and since it is a dispreferred one, the speaker uses a 'honesty phrase' with a complement like 'I don't know' to save him/her from the responsibility of being viewed negatively. When Lesley asks Phil if they invoiced him for carriage (of his goods), he replies in the negative, stating that the order is big but that he doesn't know if they put hers or not. For the latter he states, "quite honestly I: I don't kno:w" (Edwards and Fasulo, 2006: 349). The detailed emphasis on emotions is one of the strengths of DP, since the approach acknowledges and demonstrates its ubiquity in discourse, unlike the critical sociocognitive approaches.

42 Discourse and action

The 'discursive' in discursive psychology

Discourse is understood as a "functionally orientated approach to the analysis of talk and text" (Edwards and Potter, 1992: 27). Discourse analysis is largely qualitative, and the 'turn to discourse' in psychology began with the linguistic philosophical writings of Wittgenstein (1953) and later through the research on the sociology of scientific knowledge (Potter and Mulkay 1985; Ashmore 1989) and its use in social psychology (Potter and Wetherell 1987, 1988; Potter 1987). Language constitutes social reality, and discursive psychologists are interested in analysing the various versions of social reality through transcribed data, much like conversation analysts and the interrelations between the earlier two areas will be shortly explained. Discourse analysis is not viewed in the linguistic sense of discovering relations between sentences in connected speech or writing, but in the following ways:

1   The aim of discourse analysis is examining interview talk in terms of how people describe, report, remember and attribute details. This is different both from the pragmatic analysis of discourse that explicitly focusses on language structures, and from the cognitivist view of language. In DP, the focus is what happens through talk, not what is seen through language.
2   The analysis of discourse is social rather than linguistic. It deals with contextualised talk, not how something is said as part of talk. Hence, it is concerned with actual conversations, not isolated sentence analysis or textual/grammatical analysis like cohesion and coherence (Halliday and Hasan 1976).
3   Action, construction and variability (Potter and Wetherell 1987) are a part of discourse because DP analyses the various versions of people about an event, constructed in talk, and such talk is viewed as social action because people *do* things through it. Thus, talk is socially performative, and the variability of narratives highlights the constructed or functional nature of talk.
4   The rhetorical or argumentative nature of talk (Billig 1991, 1996) is crucial for understanding how people think in everyday situations and is thus an integral part of discourse analysis. For example, it is important to consider the real or potential alternative versions of someone's account to understand what his speech is aimed at – to counter, support or perpetuate some claims.
5   DP is particularly interested in analysing how cognitive knowledge and psychological categories of truth, belief, fact, error and explanation are dealt with in talk (Potter and Halliday 1990; Edwards 1991, 1999).

DP relies on CA, an approach to linguistic discourse analysis. What is telling is that the focus is not on language structures, yet the meta-meanings are derived from language. There is similarity at the functional level for both linguistic discourse analysis and DP in the sense that language performs certain functions, yet the orientation and technical terminology varies. For instance, in discourse analysis, accusing, blaming and questioning are speech acts through which meanings are derived about interaction, while in DP blaming and questioning are studied to investigate what is happening psychologically among the participants.

Conversation analysis and discursive psychology

Conversation Analysis (henceforth CA) is an approach from sociology, appropriated to discourse analysis and pragmatics, and it deals with the micro-analysis of text and talk (Sacks, Schegloff and Jefferson 1974), with its emphasis on detailed transcription of recordings of spontaneous talk. CA analyses talk to understand how humans make sense of the world around them and how they engage in meaning-making in everyday life, on the assumption that social reality is performative in nature, language is indexical and that context and language are reciprocally related. CA employs several features as part of the turn-taking mechanism to study conversations, including turn-length and distribution, adjacency pairs, preferred and dispreferred responses, types of silences, topic management and repair mechanisms.

The relevance of CA to DP can be understood from the fact that CA provides the scaffold for analysing how psychological states operate through talk as it engages in detailed, step-by-step analysis of what happens in talk. Psychology, here, can be seen as an analytic resource, enabling to uncover human psyche as voiced in interaction. As Potter and Edwards put it, "how psychological relevancies figure as members' concerns within, and for, the practices of situated talk" (2012: 702). Moreover, CA assumes intersubjectivity in talk, and this can be helpful in DP, especially in seeing how causal attribution and blaming is performed as part of talk. Talk is social practice whereby participants intersubjectively understand each other, reformulate their intent and sense of accountability, interactionally produce meanings and descriptions together with explanation of actions, and not just react to stimulus, in the behaviourist cause-effect manner, as some critics note (Edwards 1997). Thus, the use of CA procedures provides a nuanced reading of the complexity of interaction in family, social and institutional settings, if it is assumed that the psychology of persons is processed and comprehended in talk. Talk provides the basis for further action. In such an analysis, who speaks, about whom and how shows the psyche of the speaker, the person talked about and the hearer when he/she responds accordingly. In this sense, CA can provide the framework for attitude assessment through dialogue. Research (Pomerantz 1978) shows that assessments (evaluations and descriptions) is done differently for compliments and self-depreciatory remarks and that CA can throw light on the attitudes held and assessments made through detailed attention directed to the interaction process. Similarly, intention of the speaker and agency can also be understood through the semantic and grammatical structures in talk (Edwards 2008). In addition, cognitive states and intention of a person can be understood through normative talk like refusals that have a set structure comprising appreciation, mitigated refusal and account for refusal.

44 Discourse and action

Discursive psychologists, therefore, have wholly or partially employed the methodology of CA, for insightful analysis.

In fact, Potter and Edwards (2012) claim that the rich complexity of everyday talk can not only give psychological insights about the participants but cannot be accounted for by classical psychological theories. CA has also challenged the set, traditional ways of doing research in psychology in favour of more open-ended, flexible recordings of natural talk. However, CA claims (Schegloff 2005) that it is a self-contained and adequate approach and need not rely on others, but it is interesting to note that psychology's contributions to CA can lend richer insights about the mundane activity of talking. For instance, neuropsychological research on the timing of speech and brain structure correlates with word selection, repair management and especially delays in giving dispreferred responses (Pomerantz and Heritage 2012; Potter and Edwards 2012). Although CA continues to be employed by discursive psychologists due to its numerous merits, the interaction between the two disciplines is far from complete, and further research can prove the ways in which psychology is fruitful for CA.

Discursive action model

The discursive action model (DAM) is not a typical model or theory in the traditional sense, but a "conceptual scheme that captures some of the features of participants' discursive practices" (Edwards and Potter, 1992: 154). Cognitive states are construed differently in this model as compared to traditional cognitive and social psychology. In DAM, cognitive states are not revealed in language but are enacted or operate through language that makes the model actional in nature. The focus is on three aspects, each of which will be addressed in detail.

1   Action – the processes of remembering and attribution are viewed as reports (accounts, descriptions and formulations of events) and the inferences that are made as part of it. Such reports are commonly a part of activity sequences such as how to invite, refuse, blame, defend, justify, etc. In doing action, people indirectly tell about themselves, whether they are selfish, rude, cowardly, racist or otherwise, and such actions are sensitive and related to one's image (Potter 1996).
2   Fact and interest – the stake or interest of the participant is managed through the phenomenon of attribution in reports. Therefore, a report of a participant is constructed to appear as factual by using several discursive techniques and to rhetorically undermine alternative versions of the report.
3   Accountability – reports highlight how speakers deal with the interwoven issues of accountability and agency in the way they talk of their actions and those of other people, and how they pin the responsibility/blame on themselves or others. Reports specifically highlight the latter.

Memory and attribution (the process by which we judge the actions of others, favourably or unfavourably) are perceptually derived cognitive notions that are conceived in reductionist terms as mental constructs or representations in traditional social psychology (Edwards and Potter 1992). However, in DP they are recast in functional and naturalistic terms, as actions occurring in interaction or argument through text and talk. In discourse, memory is treated as what happened in an event, and the versions of these events can be multitudinous, underlining the ways in which memory is constructed. Similarly, attribution is viewed as the judgement and conclusion stated about causal relations between persons and events and how people lie, misrepresent or distort facts to suit their interests. Such interpersonal interaction occurs in the form of comments, compliments, agreements, refusals and a host of other discursive activities. In pragmatics, such actions are characterised as speech acts (Austin 1962; Searle 1969, 1979) through which people do things; however, Edwards and Potter (1992) prefer not to use the linguistic terminology, but to call it discursive action. For instance, in a police interrogation about a murder, how the accused as well as the witnesses talk of the event shows their 'versions' and their memories of it; furthermore, the manner in which they blame or accuse the other party is part of their attribution. Since all this happens as part of discourse, analysis can highlight the operation of human psychology in talk. Edwards and Potter's study (1992) on Neisser's report of John Dean's memory about President Nixon's role in suppressing his opponents in the Watergate hearings reveals that much more happened in discursive and cognitive terms than Neisser was able to analyse, that Neisser's conception of memory was problematic and that there was no neutral interpretation given by participants but specific versions of the event, having specific implications. Dean, in particular, used a variety of discursive actions (in speech and writing) to mitigate the blame, garner the support of sympathisers and deflect the blame on Nixon. Through this study, the psychologists proved that if language represented the psyche of individuals, it was through social discursive action. Thus, "language as representation" was subordinate to "language as action" (Edwards and Potter, 1992: 158).

An important feature of reporting is whose stakes or interests are indicated through such action. "People treat each other, and often treat groups, as entities with desires, motivations, institutional allegiances and biases, and they display these concerns in their reports and attributional inferences" (Ibid.) because of which it becomes important to analyse what stakes people have when they narrate reports. For example, are they trying to protect themselves, blame others, mitigate the accusation or put responsibility on someone? For these reasons, DP considers participants to be in a "dilemma of stake of interest" (Ibid.) Talk, in the court of law, is normatively oriented towards a factual description where there are two or more challenging versions of an event. Examples can also be seen in conflicting reports of students on cheating in a class test. Potter (1996) discusses the concept of 'stake inoculation' – the means through which writers manage potential accusations of having a stake in what they write – by giving an example from a newspaper where a psychiatrist claims that creative artists are tortured souls, a stereotypical view for which the newspaper can be accused. Therefore, they present the psychiatrist as being sceptical of this belief and subscribing to it

46 Discourse and action

only after reviewing many cases. Edwards and Potter (1992) discuss the various ways in which accounts can be factually constructed.

1 Category entitlements – the factuality of a report depends on category membership. People in official positions are expected to know skills relating to their positions. For example, a lawyer is expected to know verdicts on earlier cases, and a doctor (unlike a layperson) is expected to know about different diseases.
2 Vivid description – often detailed, contextualised descriptions given by speakers help to provide greater detail or "facticity" (Potter, 1996: 117) about what is going on, allowing others to re-experience the event, proving that they have good observational and memory skills and are acting as a witness.
3 Narrative – even though narration is related to description, both are quite different. Narration refers to recounting a story or experience, while description is providing details about people, events, activities, etc. The plausibility of a factual report is increased when it becomes a part of a narrative because the speaker is able to relate the event to why it took place. Narratives thus demonstrate the reconstruction of one's memory, one's psychological states, and can serve "as expressions of how people understand things" (Edwards, 1997: 288) in interaction.
4 Systematic vagueness – this is the opposite of vivid details because here the speaker systematically uses vague, unclear formulations as a form of rebuttal, as done by former British Prime Minister Margaret Thatcher in defending her stance in the act of the Chancellor's resignation letter and her relations with her ministers. The Chancellor's account presents his resignation at odds with his personal motives, whereas Thatcher uses role discourse and vague statements such as 'advisors are there to advise and ministers are there to decide' to defend herself, claiming that she did not want him to resign (Edwards and Potter 1992).
5 Empiricist accounting – in this discourse type, commonly found in scientific writing, humans are passive or secondary agents who do not 'pick up' facts; rather, facts force themselves upon them. Discursive psychologists claim that such neutral scientific knowledge is itself a construction, and DP's role lies in displaying the nature of such knowledge production.
6 Rhetoric of arguments – logical arguments or rhetorical tropes used in constructing an argument not only highlight the complex thinking of people but are themselves discursive activities through which blame and attribution of responsibility can happen. We will examine them in detail in a later chapter.
7 Extreme case formulations – these are the use of phrases and sentences that make an argument effective by employing extreme opinions/judgements about an event (Pomerantz 1978, 1984). For example, 'no one reads a printed book nowadays' or 'she has never been late for office' are evaluative ways of assessing someone's behaviour and building a strong case for, or against, them.
8 Consensus and corroboration – the factuality of a report can be greatly increased by invoking everyone's consensus on it or presenting the experience

Discourse and action **47**

as agreed upon by everyone, the witnesses or the observers. Often consensus can merge with normativity or what is socially acceptable, lending further strength to one's version. Corroboration too is quite useful for persuasive communication (Dickerson 1997).

9   Lists and contrasts – these are very commonly used in political oratory, especially the three-part list (problem, cause and solution) that develops a case as opposed to a threatening alternative.

All the above features of factual constructions indicate that reports are created rhetorically to undermine the strength of a real or potential alternative, to suit the interests of the speaker. While doing so, one learns about the speaker's attitudes and opinions (Billig 1991), and thus these features are invaluable tools for exploring one's cognitive and social reality.

Accountability, the third aspect of DAM, deals with attribution of blame or responsibility on the other, in narrating or reporting. However, in holding someone else responsible, the speaker might be held responsible; that is, there exists another level of accountability. For instance, the report writer can be held accountable for criticising and falsely implicating a minister in a case on riots. Similarly, in light of the legal procedures on sexual harassment in the workplace, a teacher might be held accountable for blaming another when he/she was innocent. Burleson (1986) analyses the talk between two teachers about the poor performance of a college student in which the teachers' talk constructs the student as the agent responsible for her academic failure even after repeated attempts by the teacher to help her.

Another aspect that is relevant for analysis is footing (Goffman 1981), which shows the orientation of the speaker and the basis on which the account is given: first-person direct experience or second-person testimony or a passer-by's observation. This indicates the level of personal accountability or distance that the speaker can maintain in constructing the report or description. Edwards and Potter (1992) discuss a newspaper report of the American bombing of an Iraqi building that led to the death of 300 persons, and the vocabulary used for its description; the Americans call it a 'military bunker' while the Iraqis label it as 'wreckage' and a 'civilian shelter,' and amidst the two conflicting views, the newspaper reporter tries to be neutral. Through this discussion, the theorists assert that often what people say is not necessarily their own; it might be another's. Similarly, when people account, blame, describe or justify, their Self is divided into many selves that might be held responsible for some action. For example, the blame for cheating on a diet by secretly eating your favourite dish might be assigned not entirely to you, but a part of you that wanted a break from the strict regime.

Discursive psychologists (Edwards and Potter 1992; Edwards 1999) assert that their action-oriented approach can provide interesting insights about psychological phenomena such as categories, role and personality. Categories refer to the social categories about persons, events and objects that allow individuals to make inferences about them and process information. For instance, an oven is used for baking (object) and a doctor is someone who is knowledgeable and who treats patients

48 Discourse and action

(person). Discursive descriptions reveal why particular categories are chosen as part of an argument and to what effect. In racist discourse, for example, the category of minority community is chosen to create a threat to the majority populace in terms of education, housing, jobs, etc. (van Dijk 1984, 2008b). Likewise, the role and personality of the speaker and the people talked about in discourse can give clues regarding the way in which the speaker frames an argument, causally attributing blame to others while in turn revealing their stake or interest.

Summing up

Although discursive psychology is an umbrella term for a conglomeration of disparate approaches to the study of psychology, the one advocated by Edwards and Potter is distinctive in several ways. Firstly, it represented a reaction against mainstream, quantitative, standardised laboratory experiments and cognitivist studies of innate mental representations of human behaviour. Secondly, the DAM model focussed on action-oriented discourse to study individuals' psychological states, and in the process they modified the meaning of discourse from an emphasis on language structures to language as a means for understanding human psyche. Thirdly, the data under study consisted of larger stretches of natural speech or social interaction, as opposed to closed ended questionnaires and scales, to understand the complexity and interrelation between speech and thought. Lastly, there are differences between DP and sociocognitive approaches like context models in terms of the emphasis on discourse and the object of study. In the latter, focus on language leads to unearthing sociopolitical issues, while in the former, the operation of psychological states and emotions is a central issue. Yet another difference is the absence of a discussion of critical issues (power and ideology) or a relativist stance in the words of Parker (2015a) that makes judgements against oppression and marginalisation very difficult since discursive psychologists emphasise the constructed nature of all discourses, treating them as mere versions of social reality. Thus, they are not sociopolitically committed as other discourse analysts (Fairclough 1989; van Dijk 2009). The model, however, offers a rigorous methodology and has wide applicability in politics, identity issues, racism, medical science and even media studies (Stier and Blomberg 2015)

Suggested reading

Articles on discursive psychology by Derek Edwards (2005) and Potter and Hepburn (2007) are useful introductions to the area. A more detailed account of the DAM model can be found in *Discursive Psychology* written by Edwards and Potter (1992). In a related work, Edwards (1997) argues for a more functional account of the operation of emotions in discourse. For a nuanced reading and application of the concepts of discursive psychology, Wiggins (2017) is quite helpful.

4

DISCOURSE, REPERTOIRES AND OUT-THERE-NESS

This chapter explicates another approach to discourse analysis by Jonathan Potter and Margaret Wetherell in their landmark work *Discourse and Social Psychology* (1987). Even though this approach falls under the broad rubric of discursive psychology, sharing its broad concerns, the researchers follow a different methodology from that of the DAM model (described in the previous chapter), and it is significant for discussion because of the following reasons. The work was written as a reaction against the trans-Atlantic traditional approaches in social psychology that valued experimental research, demanded consistency and validity in results and could not relate a social psychological analysis to broader, sociopolitical and cultural contexts. The earlier approaches could not provide an adequate explanation for causality and emphasised methodology, yet they did not provide the systematics for conducting psychological research. Potter and Wetherell's approach, influenced by post-structuralism, proposed a clear-cut methodology for researching how action happened through discourse and the conceptual tool for understanding such action – interpretative repertoires. Earlier psychological studies were mostly quantitative, were aimed at consistency in responses and were not extensively grounded in descriptive analysis. The discursive psychological approach, in contrast, was largely qualitative and observational, focussing on the constructed nature of talk through recorded transcripts or in-depth, open-ended interviews. In short, research was based not on items ticked, but on what people said and how they said it. The approach thus made use of theory, meta-theory and philosophy to understand the underlying basis of discursive action (Potter 2012).

Concept of discourse

One of the main contrasts to the earlier approaches was Potter and Wetherell's full-length discussion of discourse and its theories such as conversation analysis,

50 Discourse, repertoires and out-there-ness

speech act theory and semiotics. However, unlike Edwards and Potter (1992), they did not rely solely on conversation analysis as an empirical methodology for data collection. Discourse was described as language that:

> is used for a variety of functions and its use has a variety of consequences; language is both constructed and constructive; the same phenomenon can be described in a number of ways . . . the constructive and flexible ways in which language is used should themselves become a central topic of study.
>
> *(Potter and Wetherell, 1987: 35)*

This short definition explains the nature of discourse and its value for these social psychologists. In the spirit of speech act theory, any piece of discourse can have a variety of functions and effects upon the hearer, so the focus is on the "action and outcome oriented nature" of discourse (Potter, Wetherell, Gill, and Edwards, 1990: 207). There is no fixed interpretation of talk; in fact, the focus is on the multitudinous ways of talking and what happens through talk, relating talk to the broader sociocultural contexts. Therefore, contextual analysis assumed a wider role than what was found in traditional studies. The analysts do not begin research with cognitive assumptions but with the view of understanding social practices (Potter 2012). In addition, the emphasis is on the constructed nature of discourse or various versions of social reality, highlighting that the use of discourse involves "pre-existing linguistic resources . . . choice and selection from possibilities" (Potter et al., 1990: 207). Moreover, variability in responses is a crucial feature of discourse, as explained below.

The value of discourse studies can be understood through a critique of traditional attitude research. Earlier studies sought uniformity in responses through the use of attitude scales to measure people's attitudes, but discourse emphasises that attitudes cannot be assessed on a scalar level but through the views of people on a topic, that is, via talk or writing. Moreover, even though such scales provided a multi-dimensional view of one's attitude, they could not explain attitude variability or inconsistency in opinions, by the same person, over a period of time. The variability in measuring attitudes was "a considerable embarrassment to traditional attitude theories" (Potter and Wetherell, 1987: 54) but was valued in discourse analysis since it lent richness and complexity to the phenomenon, and Potter and Wetherell provided definite steps to study such empirical variability. In addition, no matching was sought between the attitude holder and what he/she spoke of, but discursive formulations were studied to understand the phenomenon and the speaker's attitude. So discourses were creative constructions about the social world, and the focus shifted to a closer examination of one's speech and its implications.

Another aspect of discourse is reflexivity that is explained through a rigorous critique of scientific talk and rules, a purportedly realistic and neutral domain of knowledge. Potter and Wetherell (1987) explain that there exists considerable flexibility in the way scientists express particular rules to explain their stance and critique that of others, since rules are not universally applicable. To prove their point, construct a convincing argument and to oppose rival claims, scientists can both use and criticise rules, making the opponent's stance problematic and theirs neutral or natural, and such variation and flexibility underscores the constructed nature of scientific discourse. The moot point is that even though science is claimed to be a neutral, knowledge-generating field, the presentation of scientific information is not free from the scientist's bias, beliefs, ideological leanings, relations with colleagues and institutional power, and thus scientific discourse too should be reflexively studied as constructed discourse. In fact, all discourse, narratives and accounts are subject to critical self-examination, creating rigour, clarity and systematicity in discursive psychological research.

Like Edwards and Potter (1992), Potter and Wetherell also rely on conversation analysis as a methodological approach, asserting that the richness of linguistic and paralinguistic data (intonation, word stress, lexical selection, etc.) shows the severe limitation of earlier attitude studies. Experimental studies of accounts divorced from their context highlighted how far removed the social psychologist was from the actual social setting because accounts in conversation analysis are treated as part of sequential talk, and people's accounts denote their use of preferred and dispreferred responses (questions, accusations, rebuttals, answers, etc.) in particular contexts, along with revealing power and gender relations among the participants. Thus, discursive action relies on detailed examination of conversations in their larger sociopolitical and day-to-day context to explain the talk and its ramifications.

Self and subjectivity

The concept of the Self is uni-dimensional and enduring in traditional psychological research, with personality traits "waiting to be discovered" by the analyst (Potter and Wetherell, 1987: 95). One of the earlier theories, trait theory put forward by John Eysenck (1953) and John Cattell (1966), assumed that human personality was a conglomeration of different traits, and the task of a personality inventory or test was to measure specific traits like extroversion, introversion, agreeableness and openness and to record the combination of traits. However, it was found that individual personality was not constantly dominated by a single trait, but their manifestation was situation-dependent. Moreover, individuals reacted differently in situations on the basis of not just inherent traits, but the roles (personal, social and professional) they were expected to play, such as that of a mother, a teacher, a doctor, etc. Thus, the Self was not just trait-driven but created through social roles.

In contrast, role theory (Dahrendorf 1973) postulated that individual personality varied according to the roles played by people; that is, their behaviours associated with particular roles, broadly dividing the Self as performing various public and private roles. The Self in such a case was divided into several disparate entities since discrepancy could be created between what was expected

52 Discourse, repertoires and out-there-ness

of someone and what they actually were or wanted to be. The multiple selves constructed in role theory assumed central focus in the humanistic tradition (Rogers 1951, 1957, 1961; Maslow 1968), as Rogers put forward the view that human personality was a struggle between the current self and the future self, between how one views oneself and how others view it. This dichotomy creates conflict and the struggle between the individual and society. Much of psychological analysis or therapy is a journey from actuality to aspiration, assisted by the psychologist. These theories could not sufficiently explain the Self since it cannot be limited to set personality traits and social roles. Another issue was that the Self was construed as an autonomous entity, in conflict with societal expectations and norms; whereas contemporary social thought conceives of the Self as interwoven and emerging from social actions, behaviour, knowledge and speech. The focus was not on Self-as-entity but Self constructed through interaction and talk or discourse.

The discursive Self is articulated in social practices, activities and speech and may manifest many traits, roles and beliefs that are subject to change and in contrast with each other. Thus, the Self is not a collection of heterogeneous aspects assessed by the psychologist, but a dynamic, sentient being created in and through discourse, changing according to context. Such a being is complex and can hold inconsistent attitudes. For example, one might be a feminist in certain matters and conservative in others and can hold both kinds of views for a long period of time. Research thus focusses on the "multiplicity of self-constructions and their social and interpersonal functions" (Potter and Wetherell, 1987: 103) as created through language. Studies (Harré 1983, 1985; Smith 1981) indicate that the conception of the Self in the Western world is different from indigenous cultures like that of Maoris in New Zealand. Here, the Self is not the repository and originator of all actions and practices, but individual behaviour depends on outside forces such as ritual observances for ancestors that provide *Mana* or power. Individuals do not possess enduring traits and emotions, but they are considered 'visitations' depending on the context. The Self can also be studied from the grammatical matrix and everyday conversation (Harré 1985) wherein individuals refer to themselves and others by different pronouns and deictic markers, and they also use cognitive metaphors for the same (Lakoff and Johnson 1980). Humans, in conversation, can divide themselves into subject and object, and this ability is valued by discourse analysts to understand the constructed nature of the Self. Common examples can be the use of expressions such as 'I made myself do this' or 'I have to remind myself to do this.'

The notion of a dynamic Self can become more subtle and comprehensive through a critical perspective. In discourse studies, the Self is produced not just linguistically but also socially (Althusser 1971; Foucault 1972, 1976) through the matrix of power relations and ideological beliefs. They are produced as subjects through discourse, thus subscribing to a particular discourse creates a particular kind of subjectivity for example, one's subjective experiences as suspect under police interrogation. Feminist discourse analysts (Hall and Bucholtz

Discourse, repertoires and out-there-ness **53**

1995; Mills 1995) and feminist theorists (Smith 1993) have shown that discursive talk includes understanding the subjectivities of women. Potter and Wetherell's research demonstrated the complexity and variability of identity enmeshed with power play. They conducted interviews with people regarding their opinion of the controversial New Zealand tour of South Africa, where many New Zealanders protested against the matches and Apartheid and the police were forced to intervene to subdue the riots. The researchers found that the rioters were labelled as 'trouble makers' and were divided into two groups: those with genuine intentions who wished to support the tour but were unaware of the implications of such a practice, and those who engaged in violence and aggression for the fun of it. The image of the police, on the other hand, was neutral, as those who were compelled to take measures to curb the violence, thus maintaining the status quo of power relations in society. These varied and complex images highlighted how discourse could be flexibly used to blame, praise, attack or justify people's actions and how attention to language showed not just the psyche of people but their sociopolitical leanings as well.

Interpretative repertoires

Potter and Wetherell's inspiration for discourse came partly from pragmatics but primarily from Gilbert and Mulkay's notion of interpretative repertoires which is a central feature of their approach. They describe the notion as follows:

> this is not to imply that there is no regularity at all in discourse – simply that regularity cannot be pinned at the level of the individual speaker. There is regularity in the variation. Inconsistencies and differences in discourse are differences between relatively internally consistent, bounded language units, which we have called, following Gilbert and Mulkay (1984), interpretative repertoires.
>
> *(Wetherell and Potter, 1988: 172)*

They write further that, "repertoires can be seen as building blocks speakers use for constructing versions of actions, cognitive processes and other phenomena. Any particular repertoire is constituted out of a restricted range of terms used in a specific stylistic and grammatical fashion" (Ibid.). Linguistic structure per se is not the focus, but repetitive patterns of language use are what make up the discourse. Interpretative repertoires are versions of reality that are variable, produced by different speakers in accounting for different activities and tasks. They can be recognised through the use of particular grammatical, stylistic features and figures of speech that denote a particular construction of reality, showing how people support, refute or undermine certain claims. They are explanatory resources (repetitive patterns of vocabulary, metaphors and tropes) that individuals use when talking about others and while constructing arguments, and they broadly pertain to a particular topic or theme. They are not intrinsically linked

54 Discourse, repertoires and out-there-ness

to social groups, yet each profession has certain repertoires associated with it. Repertoires help us to categorise information about people, events and happenings, which Potter (1996) claims is an essential feature of how discourse is used to talk about our environment, as can be seen later in the study on racism. Also, some individuals always use particular repertoires and others use different ones, yet analysts never assume the use of the same repertoire by an individual. Moreover, in the investigation of repertoires, analysts do not assume that language is the window for revealing cognitive entities; the "concern is firmly with *language use*: the way accounts are constructed and different functions" (Potter and Wetherell, 1987: 157, emphasis original). Thus, grammatical resources are not valued in discursive psychology as they are by linguists, yet Potter et al. (1990) argue that attention to them can be revealing, especially stereotypical tropes and language patterns. The researchers also claim that this notion is not the only tool for discourse analysis but one of the tools that can be supplemented with other discursive approaches such as conversation analysis.

The basis for Potter and Wetherell's use of interpretative repertoires is the study by Nigel Gilbert and Michael Mulkay (1980, 1984). They interviewed 34 scientists who either supported or argued against the transmission of protons across the cell wall and the role of these protons in forming a protein called ATP (adenosine triphosphate). They contrasted the scientific publications of the respondents with what they spoke in interviews, and on the basis of this contrast they labelled two repertoires: the empiricist and the contingent repertoire. Repertoires were described as the repetitive use of terms for "characterizing and evaluating actions, events and other phenomena" (Potter and Wetherell, 1987: 149). They found the following differences between the two repertoires.

1 Empiricist repertoire – this was based on the assumption that empirical phenomena was understood through actions and beliefs, without the involvement of the authors/scientists, thus creating an impression of neutrality and grammatical impersonality through structures as 'the findings point to,' 'the data suggests,' etc. (Potter 1996). Laboratory work was considered conventional, and primacy was given to experimental data and universal procedural rules as the basis of theory formation.

2 Contingent repertoire – the assumption here was that the scientist's professional actions were influenced by things/actions outside the laboratory; therefore, the actions and beliefs of the scientist were dependent on speculation, insightful thinking, social and personal ties, etc. The link between their actions/beliefs and the topic of study were not neutral and clear-cut, and the findings were presented as a dramatic revelation. In the interviews conducted, both these repertoires were used, but more so the latter.

The interesting point was the ways in which the scientists accounted for errors in the theories of other scientists, claiming their own views to be primary and, in turn, error-free. In the contingent repertoire, errors could be explained by a variety of factors: subjective bias, naivety, prejudice, personal rivalry, false intuition, reluctance in making an effort or understanding the new theory, too much reliance on an authoritative figure, dislike for change, etc. Gilbert and Mulkay found that the views of scientists were inconsistent with each other and the views of the same person too were inconsistent as scientists linked their data and conclusions in a deterministic manner – for example, 'that's how it is.' While the scientists who maintained the empiricist repertoire claimed neutrality for their findings, yet they attributed the errors to rival scientists, using the factors from contingent repertoire. The question then arose: How did the scientists resolve the conflicts springing from the use of two disparate repertoires, particularly if they became aware of such a difference? Most of them used a technique called TWOD by the researchers ('the truth will out device'), whereby the respondents claimed that scientific research would be re-evaluated and the truth of the findings would eventually surface. In this way, they were able to support empiricist determinism and yet articulate their views on the errors of their colleagues using the contingent repertoire. Thus, they could maintain two inconsistent and totally diverse repertoires and views, without compromising either and without becoming aware of the ideological dilemma. Interpretative repertoires were a useful tool in understanding the complexity and richness of human thinking.

Potter and Wetherell (1988) expanded the notion of repertoires through their investigation of racism in New Zealand between New Zealand Europeans and Maoris. This was a significant contribution, since it portrayed that language in context could manifest the interplay of social operations such as power and ideological leanings. The researchers collected enormous amounts of data from 40 women and 41 men of different political affiliation who voiced different attitudes and beliefs. Therefore, to bring consistency to their interpretation, they coded their data to find many interpretative repertoires out of which they explained three: cultural fostering, pragmatic realism and togetherness. The first repertoire was used by more than 90% of the respondents, while half the respondents employed the other two, demonstrating the variability in data. The aim of this analysis was to highlight that even though the views of New Zealanders were garbed under morality, sympathy and affiliation with Maoris, they were highly racist and sometimes offensive, showing their superiority. Cultural fostering refers to multiculturalism that accommodates both cultures, yet the respondents argued that such cultural accommodation was the duty of Maoris, and the New Zealanders just had to clear space for them, as a mother does for a child! In addition, the development of Maori culture was clearly the responsibility and problem of Maoris themselves, and pragmatic realism denoted that Maori culture was obsolete and needed to be abandoned. New Zealanders stating this view presented themselves as realistic, modern and practical, but this contradicted the repertoire that meant peaceful existence with the Maoris. Similarly, togetherness meant the mutual co-existence of both races, yet the picture was not that simple since the normative culture was that of New Zealanders, and the respondents

56 Discourse, repertoires and out-there-ness

implied that the Maoris should stop inciting conflict and war and learn to live peacefully with their conquerors. This study proved how the focus on language use demonstrated the genuine intentions of New Zealanders and their underlying racist prejudice. Their responses were multi-layered and could not be called overtly oppressive or racist, yet there was inconsistency in them together with a covert streak of discrimination. The subtlety and complexity of "lay explanations as they are deployed in natural contexts" (Wetherell and Potter, 1988: 183) and their analysis could provide penetrating insights about a wide variety of social and psychological phenomena through language. Thus, unlike the DAM model, interpretative repertoires were a suitable tool for combining sociopolitical issues with psychology.

Methodology

Potter and Wetherell (1987) discuss the steps to conduct discourse analysis, favouring a qualitative, systematic methodology guided by practical considerations. For ease of understanding, the steps will be numbered.

1 The research question should engage in a micro-analysis of talk on a mundane or important topic, and the focus should be on construction and function of talk.
2 Since discourse analysis is an intensive process, the sample size need not be large as required in quantitative studies that make use of statistical tests. Sometimes one interview or even ten can suffice if detailed amounts of data are collected through them. Also, collection of data from multiple sources on a particular topic is preferable but not obligatory.
3 The sources can be conversations, news reports, official documents, letters, etc., and while collecting the data, practical and ethical considerations are relevant.
4 Though natural talk is preferred, interviews are a significant source of data because of the intervention of the researcher. The questions should be designed in an open-ended manner, serving a functional purpose, and they should not aim solely for consistency but celebrate variation in responses.
5 The transcription of the responses should be detailed, readable and lengthy, paying attention to minor details such as pauses, hesitation and word stress.
6 The next stage is the coding of data that should cover as much variation and as many odd or borderline cases as possible to present a representative view of the sample and the phenomena.
7 Doing analysis requires skill in interpreting the transcripts and in finding systematic patterns in the data. This aspect will be dealt later.
8 The analysis should aim for validity in the following ways. It should seek to explain both macro- and micro-levels of analysis, relate to the actual social lives of people, explain and solve new problems that surface as part of the analysis and be fruitful in terms of providing novel explanations for phenomena.

Discourse, repertoires and out-there-ness **57**

9 The final report is not a summing up of the findings but an explication and validation of the analysis, putting the focus on the analytical procedures and the discourse itself.
10 The last stage is applicability of the research, and one of the ways is popularisation, that is, publishing the findings for the general public in an easy, palatable manner not just for academicians.

Wetherell (1998) expands on the analytic procedures, arguing that conversation analytic-oriented discourse analysis is not the only kind of analysis preferred in discursive psychology. Rather, critical analysis relying on Foucauldian and ideological notions is also relevant because the latter provides a detailed examination of the subject positions offered to participants, just like the former gives insights into the micro-level of talk. Thus, the need for a two-sided analytical process: both post-structuralist discourses and conversation analytic techniques are useful for analysis, a view reinforced by Potter (1996). Through the analysis of men's talk, Wetherell and Edley (1999) highlight how several interpretative repertoires are used in conversation such as masculinity, sexuality as performance and achievement, heteronormativity, alcoholism, etc.; and by talking on such varied topics, the participants go through diverse subject positions, knowledge of which can enhance analysis. The researchers identified three subject positions corresponding to the repertoires of the speakers, that is, how they described themselves and their relation to hegemonic masculinity: heroic, ordinary and rebellious. In the first case, the men identified themselves as in control of people and situations; in the second, they described themselves as ordinary or average in contrast to the stereotypical notions of masculinity; and in the third, their identity emerged in contrast to hegemonic masculinity by being unconventional or resistant to conformity. The analysis revealed how masculinity was a set of negotiated, iterative, discursive practices found through the repertoires used by the men. Gender was a way of self-presentation, and the procedures through which men live, talk and behave in masculine ways are psychological and discursive, hence the term psycho-discursive. In talk, men momentarily reveal their emotions, intentions, beliefs and other psychological states; thus, psycho-discursive practices situated men's talk as local, global, variable and patterned, highlighting the ways in which men subjectify themselves, linking the reproduction of the social to the psychological, and gender to psyche.

Unlike the DAM model, analysis cannot just be dependent on local meaning-making, as Schegloff (1997) proposes, but needs to look at the broader context and identity issues offered by post-structuralist discourse analysis (Laclau and Mouffe 1985/2001). Exploring the tensions and contradictions in discourse and understanding why and how people talk explains the social and cultural significance of their speech, their behaviours and identity. In short, discourse is seen as a meaning-making activity that lends a more productive sense to the participants' orientation; their subject positions throw light on the multiple ways in which they are constituted in discourse and how discourse shapes society. This

58 Discourse, repertoires and out-there-ness

is particularly the case with ideological analysis that interpellates and creates subject positions, for they can tell us how subjects are created in and through discourse (Althusser 1971; Parker 2017). Therefore, analysis in social psychology favours an eclectic approach, using concepts and notions from varied fields for fruitfulness and coherence.

Emotion and psycho-discursive practices

Another related issue is of emotion, with researchers acknowledging that they are complex, socioculturally specific terrains (Potter 2012). Earlier studies conceived affect as inchoate and intense emotions that escape or exceed language (Massumi 1995, 2002) felt and experienced sub-verbally. The researchers thus created a binary between discourse and affect and between the speaking and feeling subject. However, Wetherell argues for an integration of discourse and affect studies in situated activity that throws light on how individuals feel, think and speak in social contexts. She (2008) asserts that subjectivity is a complex phenomenon that can be understood through psycho-discursive practices – collective and socially organised ways of signifying and talking about emotions and other psychological states like intentions and motivations. Affect needs to be located within "subjects and objects, individual and collective bodies" (Wetherell, 2012: 159), like a practice that socially constitutes the subject. Wetherell (2013) advocates a fine-grained analysis of affect to understand the textured lives of humans within a matrix of power, ideology and society, rather than viewing it as a feature of excess (Brennan 2004). Affective practice explains how emotions are embodied and how they operate, and qualitative research can help to understand this process, for it analyses in depth the ways in which people speak, for instance through the use of conversation analysis. Wetherell and Edley (1999) give a notable demonstration of psycho-discursive practices in use in the study of masculinity where the respondents employ the psychological process of identification as a discursive accomplishment (Wetherell and Edley 1999). In yet another fine-grained analysis (Wetherell and Edley 1997) of boys' talk and their self-professed relations to masculinity, the researchers argue that masculinity and its associated psychological processes are discursively performed and enacted. The boys in the sample initially criticised the more masculine boys in their college, known as the 'hard lads' for their aggression, virility and physical prowess; yet, ironically, later they seemed to agree with the traditional notion of masculinity and its associated traits, like the 'hard lads.' In a later study, Wetherell and Edley (2014) argued that examining the "patchwork texture of everyday masculinities in situ" (2014: 360) was crucial for understanding the ideological nature of gender identities which could be possible through a discursive psychological framework, not an experimental, empirical one as found in earlier studies. Moreover, the responses of the men highlighted a multiplicity of imaginary identities and identifications that could not have been explained through psychometric research using scales and inventories that required closed-ended

Discourse, repertoires and out-there-ness **59**

replies. In the former, the participant is the social actor who is actively, psychologically and discursively involved in constructing his identity in valid ecological situations. Therefore, not just the cognitive, but the emotional-attitudinal aspect of men's talk becomes relevant, making psycho-discursive practices a useful notion in studying the intersections of affect, gender and ideology. The study of affect and discourse is a significant contribution by Wetherell because it clearly shows that everyday language and interpersonal relations are imbued with how one feels. The individual is a sentient, thinking, feeling creature, involved in multiple social relations, presenting a complex and varied picture of one's identity. Most CDA theorists like Fairclough (1992) overlook the fact that one's psychology, especially emotions, shape one's identity, and often the dynamics of power in interpersonal interaction can be linked to one's emotions and other psychological states. Context models, in contrast, provide a better view of human behaviour incorporating one's thinking and feeling as part of everyday interaction. However, their treatment of language varies. Wetherell's approach focusses more on coding of language patterns, while van Dijk stresses detailed language analysis to understand social interaction.

Constructing out-there-ness

An integral part of narratives is the representation of reality; who is presented in what way because of which reasons. Discursive constructions produce various versions that create boundaries of inclusion and exclusion, becoming sites of power play and ideological clash. Like CDA theorists (Chouliaraki and Fairclough 1999) who rely on language to analyse ideology and power, Potter (1996) too claims that reality can be changed through language use, and in the following techniques, DP comes close to CDA in terms of its focus on language and the constructed nature of discourse.

1   Categorisation and ontological gerrymandering – specific vocabulary items can demonstrate the ways in which persons, events, objects and actions are constituted. This can be done through the use of metaphors (Lakoff and Johnson 1980) and nominalisation (Kress and Hodge 1979; Fairclough 1989) whereby a verb is made into a noun and agency is avoided. For example, instead of saying 'the mob attacked the man,' one can say 'the attack on the man,' thus removing all agency from the statement. Ontological gerrymandering refers to how some facets of an argument are accentuated while others are avoided due to the vested interests of the dominant party. For example, Potter, Wetherell and Chitty (1991) asserted that the argument developed by a television programme on cancer charity centred on how the money was used for research instead of helping the cancer patients. Other issues such as improved survival of patients, prevention of the disease and quality of life of cancer victims were also part of the argument, but their presentation varied in sequence.

60 Discourse, repertoires and out-there-ness

2   Extrematisation and minimization – when people justify their actions, they can use extreme-case formulations (Pomerantz 1984) such as 'never,' 'always,' 'completely,' 'every,' 'extremely,' etc., just as they can minimise the force of an account by using polar opposites of these words. For example, a traumatic divorce of a person can be blandly, emotionlessly described as 'a little problem' (Vaillant 1977). Similarly, descriptions of violence can be maximised or minimised depending on the words that can be used (Potter 1996).

3   Normalisation and abnormalisation – this deals with the ways in which accounts are made to appear normal and abnormal. Foucault's *History of Sexuality* (1976) systematically describes the social, educational, legal and medical discourses that categorised and classified abnormal behaviour as opposed to what was socially acceptable. Another example cited by Potter (1996) is Dorothy Smith's (1993) account of K as mentally ill. When K was asked to help her friend Angela in garden work, she helped for hours, without stopping. This sets up a contrast – it is not normal to do gardening for a long time, thus K's long hours of work reflect her abnormal behaviour.

A central issue in representation is the obfuscation of agency that allows for impersonalisation and neutrality, absolving the participant of being accountable for what was said or written. In critical terms, it is significant for investigation because a lack of agency can be used to misrepresent, dominate and manipulate reality (Fairclough 1992). Out-there-ness is a ubiquitous phenomenon found in various contexts of literature, everyday talk, institutional settings and the manoeuvring of agency highlights the interplay of individual psyche, social norms and power relations in society. In discursive psychology, Potter (1996) refers to it as out-there-ness where it appears that "the description is independent of the agent" (1996: 150) and their stake.

There are many ways in which neutrality of discourses can be maintained. It can be done through impersonal constructions as found in the media, where it appears that the news reporters are only reporting the views of others. Phrases like 'was believed to be,' 'sources say that' and 'X said on the basis of anonymity' are often seen in media reports. In CDA, obfuscation is also done through nominalisations. Phrases such as 'the data supports,' 'the figures reveal' and 'the results show' highlight the use of evidential support for one's claims. Moreover, the use of witness accounts produces consensus and corroboration, lending veracity to their description because in such cases the witness is speaking as the reporter of the event(s), as opposed to a general description. Wooffitt (1992) reports that when people produce extraordinary descriptions, they often quote others, even though the quotes should not be read as actual quotes, a process known as active voicing. The use of 'they said' is a common device to provide a gist of the experiences of others, simultaneously establishing objectivity. In addition, the narrative device of focalisation or point of view (Genette 1980) produces detailed descriptions. It can be created from the viewpoint of a particular person (internal focalisation), or a general description of scenes, not the affect of characters

Discourse, repertoires and out-there-ness **61**

(external focalisation). In literary writings, the description of what characters think and feel is part of the former, while descriptions of natural scenery is a part of the latter.

A related issue is of the use of vagueness in a text which illustrates some important function performed by the speaker, like complaining, agreeing and concealing information. Potter (1996) argues that idiomatic expressions are typically vague but are employed for specific purposes in a text, to explain the feelings of the speaker and their perspective. If you say for your colleague whom you are jealous of, 'she has bitten more than she can chew,' it shows negative feelings of insecurity, envy and a sense of gloating over the other's predicament. Yet another issue is factual accounts found in history books where particular narratives are created and warranted while others are avoided to support and sustain fictional narratives and myths, and the breakdown of such grand narratives is the focus of postmodernism (Lyotard 1979/1984). For example, feminists often argue that history is his-story, downplaying the achievements of women as found in the Indian freedom struggle. Lastly, Potter (1996) argues that the details of a narrative are more important than its general structure. For instance, in court cases, the ways in which the answers of witnesses are controlled (where to start, pause and stop) is more significant than their narratives since controlling tactics decide what constitutes as the witness's speech/answer (Molotch and Boden 1985).

Summing up

Like the DAM model, Potter and Wetherell's work (1987) represents another pioneering strand in discursive psychology, broadly sharing the assumptions and methodological practices, like its reliance on conversation analysis to examine the sphere of psychology in discourse, its anti-cognitivist, constructivist stance and its treatment of all discourses, even scientific, as factual constructions. However, the theorists differ in their views on language, especially their use of interpretative repertoires. The latter extends the meaning of discourse by its emphasis on the repeated use of grammatical and stylistic features in people's talk and writing. Also, similar to linguistic discourse analysts (van Dijk 2008a, 2009), they emphasise the issues of variability, flexibility and reflexivity in research. However, the repertoires are thematic, and one of the primary aims is to reveal all kinds of psychological states. A crucial difference from Edwards and Potter (1992) is that they do not have a relativist stance but engage in some form of critical ideological analysis of social issues like racism and draw on psychoanalytic vocabulary to understand gender, especially in Wetherell's works, thus making discursive psychology socially and culturally more relevant.

Suggested reading

The seminal work by Potter and Wetherell (1987) explains their stance and the notion of interpretative repertoires. An article by Wetherell and Potter (1988)

62 Discourse, repertoires and out-there-ness

on interpretative repertoires in the discourses of racism is a lucid exposition of the application of discursive psychology. Wetherell (2012) also explains the importance of studying affect in discourse and interaction. There are other writings that can highlight the relation between theory and practice. Potter (1996) examines social constructionism and postmodernism in relation to the construction of reality. Antaki (1994) gives a brilliant description of how explanations and arguments are used by people in representing reality. In addition, a reader on the theory and practice of discourse is Wetherell, Taylor and Yates (2001), an advanced guide that contains seminal articles and debates about the study of discourse.

5

RHETORIC AND IDEOLOGICAL DILEMMAS

Rhetoric and communication

Rhetoric, commonly known as the art of persuasive speaking or effective communication, finds its origins in Greco-Roman times, when political/public matters were discussed and decided in state assemblies through deliberations, debates and reasoning, and when anyone who wished to climb the social and professional ladder had to master the fundamentals of oratory and argument (Billig 1991). In contemporary times, the study of rhetoric has applicability in politics, advertising, discourse, narratology and conversation, for it is essentially a way of communication and argument construction (Condor, Tileaga and Billig 2013). In fact, van Dijk (1985) is of the view that the development of discourse as an interdisciplinary field can be traced back to rhetoric and *grammatica*. Thus, this chapter will deal with the notion of rhetoric and argumentation as developed by Michael Billig. Even though Billig does not provide a ready-made model or manual on rhetorical analysis, his notions offer compelling possibilities on how analysis can be done. They can be incorporated with other tools from social psychology and discourse analysis for wider applicability and greater insights on a topic. Moreover, Billig's writings on ideological dilemmas indirectly focus on language use in rhetoric; therefore, he represents yet another perspective in psychology that draws attention to the theme of discourse and communication.

Rhetorical psychology and thinking

The approach developed by Billig is known as rhetorical psychology, for it deals with ways of thinking and arguing together with the analysis of the dynamic process of reasoning to reveal conflicting ideological points of view. His approach

64 Rhetoric and ideological dilemmas

can be viewed as an alternative to the standard psychological approaches to reasoning, attitudes and ideological analysis (Billig 1991; Condor, Tileaga and Billig 2013). Aristotle's classic work *Rhetoric* exemplifies this tradition, where the writer discusses several issues such as persuasive and presentation skills in public, the employment of strong reasoning and/or emotional appeals in an argument, and their position (beginning, middle or end) to convince the listeners. As opposed to these structural pointers for rhetoric and the traditional image of the orator who aimed to suppress alternative opinions, Billig (1991, also 1987/1996) delves more on the two-sidedness of an argument and its inherent contradictions, drawing from the Sophist, Protagoras. Protagoras noticed in courts of law that a case could be argued convincingly both ways. Greeks and Romans believed that rhetoric was a powerful tool in the hands of the Athenian youth, capable of subverting the moral order of those times, and Billig asserts that similar fears exist regarding the nature of communication.

One of the most unique features of Billig's (1991) approach is that it is antithetical to the information-processing approaches where individuals engage in decision-making after considering all the alternatives. Due to excess of information, individuals selectively attend to stimuli and use procedural rules (Atkinson and Shiffrin 1968; Billig and Tajfel 1973) to understand everyday contexts, highlighting the normative nature of their thinking. For example, in most Indian colleges and universities, the teacher is supposed to dress and behave in a culturally appropriate manner, be knowledgeable and not fumble while delivering lectures, while the students are supposed to listen attentively and ask relevant questions. The fact that this typical procedure is followed in most classrooms shows how normative thinking becomes a practiced norm. If a teacher is unconventional in appearance and teaching, understanding their unconventionality requires newer ways of thinking, for creating rules and flouting them is done through complex contemplation.

Argumentative thinking

Billig (1991, 1996) proposes that thinking is not a rule-governed process as conceived by most psychologists. Psychology is primarily concerned with thinking, especially problem-solving and finding solutions, suggesting that once the problem is solved, there is no need for further thought; this is not the case, as found in common cases of freedom, justice, ethics and prejudice where the arguments can be endless and the perspectives multiple. For example, the political problem of unemployment can be argued from many perspectives, and it does not have a single, simple solution. Similarly, an argument has two basic meanings: a debate of opinions between two people and a "single piece of reasoning" (Billig, 1991: 44), where the latter is related to the former in such a way that when one person follows a line of reasoning, the others provide arguments, counter-arguments and justifications supporting their views and criticising those of the other. Billig likens thinking to an argument or debate, calling it a complex and performative process where individuals are involved in a dialogue within themselves, silent or aloud, as is portrayed by the Sophist Greek tradition.

> The thinker is the student or scholar, working within a cultural tradition which is enriched by every new insight . . . The distinctions made by these scholars are not psychological divisions made in the structure of the mind itself, but are distinctions in the sort of knowledge which can constitute the content of the mind.
>
> *(Billig, 1987: 169)*

Multiple meanings and options are weighed in the mind as part of socially shared knowledge, and they are debated upon, signifying the argumentative nature of the mind. For example, one considers the advantages and disadvantages of marital life and singlehood in arriving at the decision to marry. The minute we begin to perceive one line of thinking as more favourable, for instance single-hood and lack of commitment, our mind is already caught in the argumentative loop. Research (van Dijk 1985) indicates that prejudiced thinking is argumenta-tive, since the person will align to those aspects against the target community members that conform to their beliefs. In fact, to create an argument we rely on our presuppositions and social beliefs, thus highlighting that argumentative thinking is very much a part of everyday life as it is a part of political and media discourses. The image of the thinker "has been transformed into something more *dynamic and social* (even antisocial). It is the image of an argumentative debater . . ." (Billig, 1991: 45, emphasis mine). Our thinking is rooted in our social beliefs and cultural patterns, and whenever we choose to support a course of thinking or perceive some details at the cost of others, we are involved in arguing and thinking simultaneously. John Shotter calls this the 'way of disputa-tion.' In this manner we "learn to find our 'way around' within the landscape of complicated, indeterminate, human expressive activities – able to move both 'upstream' and 'downstream' as we conduct our inquiries" (Shotter, 2014: 60). Everyday life provides ample opportunities and problems that can be understood through argumentative thinking, the "useful, two- or more sided performative resources" (Shotter, 2014: 66). He claims that Billig's approach is not a step-by-step toolkit for the analysis of an argument, but it provides us with a new line of thinking of how we relate or orient ourselves to others and issues in our environment.

Billig's approach is notable for the following reasons. His emphasis on argu-mentative thinking and Quintilian's Principle of Uncertainty (1996) cautions us to not ignore the specifics of each situation in order to find patterns. Like the approaches by Potter and Wetherell and by van Dijk, Billig too values variabil-ity and complexity in each context. Another reason for its significance is that it links our thinking to the creation of discourses and the outside world. We argue and think, favouring what we want and what we want to see, a dynamic social process, common not just in academic discourse but in everyday social

66 Rhetoric and ideological dilemmas

contexts. Lastly, it hints at the construction of inner discourses with ourselves in the process of thinking, and therefore it extends the meaning of discourse as not something limited to external speech or writing but as interiorised language.

Aids in analysing arguments

Although there is no readymade toolkit, Billig does provide us subtle pointers that can be helpful for analysis. Firstly, the argumentative nature of thinking can be gauged from the ordinary use of words and their semantic meanings since the "connections between things have become embodied in the semantic structure of words" (Billig, 1991: 44). Thus, discourse and its meanings have not been explicitly discussed by Billig in his approach, yet discursive tools such as vocabulary, sentence structure, speech acts and prosodic and intonational features can aid in the analysis of one's thinking process. How we think, speak and write is intricately related to what we think, speak and write, and therefore discourse analysis is relevant for rhetorical analysis. Secondly, we cannot understand a piece of argument if we do not delve into its contrary argument and wider controversy. Any argument is developed on the basis of counter-positions, and knowledge of these is essential to know what is rejected and why. For example, developing an argument against the practice of *Sati* in India (where a woman burnt herself on the pyre of her husband) requires understanding the larger social, historical, economic, cultural and religious implications of such an act and even the arguments in its favour, even though one might not agree with them.

Thirdly, humans possess the capacity to resist any argument by inventing counter-arguments, just like Protagoras discovered in legal cases. Critical thinking skills come to the aid of humans, preventing them from becoming passive recipients of the orator's argument and to fully agree with him. Thus, critical analysis of an argument helps to question what the speaker is saying and why is he saying so, limiting his persuasive powers. It also explains the overall argumentative context. Fourthly, Billig (1996) discusses historical examples from Aristotle's and Protagoras's times and how strategies were provided to understand arguments and in turn served as basic building blocks of thinking. Aristotle's *Topica* proposed that strategies of thinking occurred in pairs of opposites where each strategy had a counter or negation. The psychological process of categorisation shows how persons, events and objects are labelled in relation to others for a better understanding of the world; however, for each categorisation, label or term, there exists another counter label, and the choice of a marker shows one's attitudes or thinking process and forms the basis for an argument. For instance, Bhagat Singh was a revolutionary, freedom fighter and martyr for the Indians but a seditionist and terrorist for the British government in India. Here it is important to notice the similarities and differences of both sides of an argument, what we agree to and what we don't, giving attention to its lexis. Billig's approach to rhetoric (1996) indicates that the discourse of society, cultural and historical, is a fluid, flexible interpretative field because there are always other voices, other

Rhetoric and ideological dilemmas **67**

positions and other viewpoints than the one being presented, something that was also argued by Foucault, albeit in a different manner. As Billig states, "there is always more that can be said" (1987: 256). Attention to those other voices can change the way in which we see others and ourselves, and once again language analysis helps in this regard.

Fifthly, there are many ways of constructing an argument (in speech or writing), linking discourse to one's psychology. Shotter (2014) states that objectivity in an argument arises if one believes that the sole aim of language is to represent the world in a decontextualised manner and that the world is a logical place with no contradictions or problems. However, if one believes in the multidimensional and complex nature of the world, one would realise that objectivity springs from adhering to one dimension. For example, women who believe in total patriarchal submission to the husband cannot or do not think that there is an alternative way of living, with self-respect and healthy discussion or debate with the spouse. Or, those who believe in the concept of only one life do not think of reincarnation as a long journey of the soul and this life as part of it. The way an argument is created misleads us into believing in a particular order of things, and it is this view that Billig wishes to dismantle by advocating the exploration of contradictions and opposing viewpoints. Thus, attention to discourse can reveal what is unsaid and the inherent contradictions in an argument.

Sixthly, if our strategies for arguing are the building blocks of thinking, then Billig (1991, 1996) proposes that one's thinking has the structure of a public argument or deliberative oratory, the difference being that in oratory one is arguing with another, but here one is arguing with oneself, split into two: in "observing debates, we are observing the structure of thinking itself" (1991: 49). For the purpose of analysis, it is relevant to observe how one creates an argument, justifies positions and criticises counter-positions, and this varies according to situation because, according to the ancient Greeks, every argument is unique. Thinking is not rule-governed, yet rules arise from arguments and themselves give rise to arguments, as can be seen in court cases where lawyers cite previous verdicts and cases to build a case and sometimes develop rules from their arguments. Billig (1996) cites examples from *The Talmud* (Jewish scriptures) that is a collection of rules on the right conduct in life, yet each rule becomes an argument for the Rabbis as they argue over its meaning and interpretation. One's attitudes and opinions can be performed in discourse (Puchta and Potter 2002, 2004) as a form of evaluation and attack of other's attitudes as is often seen in parliamentary debates and political speeches, though the investigators examined the issue in focus-group talks. In doing so, the speaker considers the counter-arguments and formulates points to justify their stance, while negating the other, mirroring its argumentative nature. In fact, Potter (1996) is of the view that the argumentative nature of thinking can also be seen in the construction of factual accounts. Such accounts cannot be treated as rhetorically persuasive; rather, the varied versions of an account and the tensions among them can highlight the discursive strategies used to persuade people through these versions.

68 Rhetoric and ideological dilemmas

Lastly, an aspect of argumentation involves flexibility to tailor one's views in opposition to another. Billig's study of the views of the British public on the royal family (1991, 1992) showed that in one family, the father held very strong views against the royal family and constantly argued with his kin about them. However, in his arguments he was not always against the royalty but also voiced his views as a defender of British values, overall adhering to his stance against the British monarchy. This study highlighted that individuals can either possess a singular/factual view or a multi-subjective perspective with competing values to prove their point. Thus, in many ways Billig hints that an analysis of arguments and their language would be fruitful for understanding how an argument is developed cognitively. In short, a link is forged between discourse and psychology.

Ideological dilemmas

The notion of ideological dilemmas is a notable contribution by Billig and his colleagues (1988) which stands in stark contrast to the way thinking and conversation is viewed by social psychologists. In traditional Marxist theory, ideology is explained as false consciousness that keeps one away from reality. In later works (Althusser 1971), ideology was an imaginary relationship of the individual to society and humans were passive beings who followed rituals to believe in a particular ideology. However, Billig et al. (1988) were interested not in critiquing these conceptions of ideology and the social structure that gave rise to it, but in presenting how thinking was ideological, especially commonsensical thinking. When people spoke, they exhibited an ideological paradox, rehearsing "old commonly shared stereotypes . . . reproducing conflicting conceptions contained within common sense" (Billig, 1991: 21). In other words, thinking contained contrary themes or dilemmatic views of ideology, for ideological beliefs and leanings were not voiced in a vacuum but were part of larger social patterns. Billig et al. (1988) sought to explore the patterns of thinking through ideological dilemmas. Before we delve further into this notion, it is important to state that ideological dilemmas manifest variability in thought, exposing its argumentative nature, thereby linking ideology to thinking. This is relevant because an individual's thoughts and beliefs can contradict or overlap as part of one or more ideologies, and the same person can hold inconsistent ideologies at the same time, highlighting the complex texture of cognition and ideology in everyday life.

Billig firmly asserts that one's thinking and other mental states "are themselves socially created" (1991: 14), and therefore one's internal processes can be studied as social constructions. Language plays a fundamental role in this, for it is one's discourse that gives a peek into one's psychology. Citing Marx and Engels from *The German Ideology*, he asserts that language is a form of practical consciousness that explicates the connections between one's thinking and social processes (Marx and Engels 1970; Billig 1991), an aspect that has been extensively explored by critical discourse analysts (Fairclough 1989; van Dijk 1998) by

Rhetoric and ideological dilemmas **69**

relating discourse, ideology and cognition. Ideological dilemmas are not inhibiting features of cognition but enabling aids that help individuals to articulate their thoughts, form opinions and adhere to certain social belief and practices – in other words, to understand the world.

Nature of dilemmas

A dilemma involves a choice between alternatives, and such dilemmas surface in the conversations of people when they talk about social events, persons and objects. Robin Lakoff (1973/1975) aptly summarises such a dilemma when she argues that language is sexist against women; not only does language portray women in a negative light, but women's language use depicts their powerlessness. Women are implicitly instructed to not be too loud but not even be too submissive, not to be frank but at the same time not to be quiet, "so a girl is damned if she does, damned if she doesn't" (Lakoff, 1973: 48). Another example can be a morning scene where you are getting late for the office and have to make your breakfast and complete a report that has to be submitted to the boss. This creates a dilemma of what to do first, and you can consider several alternatives like ordering a takeaway breakfast, calling your neighbour for help to type the report, making an excuse regarding why the assignment could not be prepared, etc. Everyone encounters such dilemmas on a daily basis, and what makes the decision significant is that it can change one's course of living and perception. Laboratory experiments on dilemmas study the subject's choices in terms of payoffs for a single utility, that is, money or points. The wider social significance of making choices and their repercussions has been reduced to the act of pressing buttons in a laboratory that ignores the network of social relations, values, images, beliefs and representations in which in dilemmas are embedded and manifested. Dilemmas thus represent the conflicts of common sense. As Billig et al. note, "if common sense did not possess this quality, then the dilemmas of choice could not arise with the full force of moral and social dramas" (1988: 19).

A related issue is that of language. Dilemmas are often expressed through speech and writing, and attention to specific vocabulary items can reveal them. Political speeches often draw on multiple and conflicting meanings of terms like 'freedom,' 'liberty' and 'justice' to evoke different responses from the audience. Women's magazines employ a different language to show the dilemmatic nature of ideologies: preference to surgical intervention for body sculpting versus healthy weight loss through exercise and diet (Jeffries 2007). Similarly, the dichotomy between tradition and modernity and the options available for a bride in terms of wedding appearance has been expressed in several magazine issues. Not just vocabulary, but even other discursive tools can provide insights about the nature of bridal dilemmas such as speech acts employed by the speaker and their function in the discourse, the use of modal verbs and sentence structure (Glapka 2014; Sharma 2018). The qualitative analysis of themes and counter-themes in discourse is a much-valued practice of psychologists, highlighting that

70 Rhetoric and ideological dilemmas

even though Billig does not provide a guide on discourse analysis, he understands its significance for psychologists (Potter and Wetherell 1987; Edwards and Potter 1992).

Billig et al. argue that an analysis of such dilemmas can reveal the argumentative nature of commonsensical thought. When discussing alternatives, people exhibit their internal debates, linking dilemmas to thinking. Not only this, people's thinking contains arguments that they favour and those they don't as part of being a member of a social network, but people mostly prefer consistency in beliefs. In fact, the existence of attitudes and value systems shows that people adhere to their beliefs, and the slightest opposition creates dissonance (Festinger 1957). For example, a person who is against the idea of child labour would feel extremely uncomfortable employing a child as house help and would go to any lengths to preserve his thinking. Even though schematic constructs exist (Bartlett 1932; Schank and Abelson 1977) that provide cognitive scaffolding to understand the environment, thinking is a much more complex process that goes beyond it.

Dilemmas can be broadly subdivided into explicit and implicit aspects. The former refers to the process of explicitly stating one's views and thoughts as found in parliamentary debates. Attention should be given to discursive strategies through which conflicting themes are presented and "the evocation of one value will ease the expression of the contrasting value" (Billig et al., 1988: 22). This is more of a surface-level reading of discourse in which explicit items are noticed and analysed, yet as one attempts to analyse against the grain, one is moving in the direction of implicit dilemmatic aspects. As Potter and Wetherell (1987, 1988) revealed in their study of racism in New Zealand, even though the explicit discourse of the respondents upheld multiculturalism and accommodation of Maoris, implicitly it considered the White race superior and demanded conformity from Maoris. In discursive terms, implicit aspects can be gauged from negation markers and connectives (Levinson 1983).

Types of ideology and dilemmas

Since ideological dilemmas are voiced in discourse, ideology is understood not only in terms of grand social and political narratives but even everyday naturalised assumptions. There is no single ideology, but the cross-currents of several ideologies that impinge upon one's thought processes. The mundane and the significant are both ideological, and an individual's life is permeated with two kinds of ideologies: lived and intellectual ideology. Lived ideology is "society's way of life" (Billig et al., 1988: 27) that is synonymous with culture: one's traditions, customs, patterns, beliefs and way of living as a whole, constituting 'common sense' in a particular society. In contrast, intellectual ideology is a formalised consciousness or philosophy, providing a high degree of internal consistency to thinking. For example, in any kind of feminist interpretation, the roles of gender and patriarchy would be integral aspects for understanding the context. Also,

Rhetoric and ideological dilemmas **71**

boundaries are blurred between the ideologies of routine life and that of high philosophy, each being permeated by the other. For instance, one might believe in socialism, yet in everyday living one's conduct and activities go against socialist beliefs, creating ideological dilemmas. Hence, ideologies are not just internally consistent beliefs but contain dilemmatic elements that can be a source for deliberation and debate, and rich insights can be provided if one analyses the conflicting themes in both types of ideologies. For instance, what happens when the ideology of individualism clashes with beliefs on social responsibility, humanitarianism and justice? Are not ideological dilemmas produced? (Billig et al. 1988). An examination of individualism would necessitate an examination of its themes and contrary themes, its discourses and counter-discourses, emphasising that thinking is complex, enabling, constraining and socially perceptive. In short, ideological dilemmas are fundamental to our sociocultural fabric.

Radley and Billig (1996) analyse the health dilemmas of patients, arguing that the views of the participants represent their individual opinions and simultaneously the ways in which health is constructed and understood in society. This involves examining people's private and public accounts on health. People don't just talk about health, but they construct their identity and their relationships with others through conversations on health by claiming, justifying, accusing, attributing and re-affirming their beliefs. In other words, health is both an ideological and dilemmatic topic, and speakers employ various strategies in their arguments. In interviewing a couple where the husband had undergone surgery, the researchers found that that though the wife criticised the 'naughty' husband who transgressed by doing physical activity which he was not supposed to do (like chopping wood), it is argued that he was a hero and physical exertion was good for his health, in contrast to the common medical view advising rest postsurgery. In this jointly constructed tale of the couple, not only does the conversation bespeak of the construction of shared memory, the discourse of heroism and the moral legitimacy of the wife as the anxious caretaker, but it also portrays how individuals who are ill construct health and illness, that is, how they view themselves after their sickness. The body is implicated in the way it appears and the way it is talked about. Thus, there are implications for health recovery – how patients can care for themselves, how they treat themselves as normal and how they display good health, even in sickness. In addition, when people tell their stories, they relate personal accounts with public views (talk on medical topics and attitudes towards medical authorities), and the ways in which they justify or account for their views shows a merger of 'private' and 'public' narratives and their personal ideologies.

The dialogic unconscious

Billig (1997, 2004) extends the themes and principles of discursive psychology by linking it to Freudian psychoanalytic theory, emphasising the nature of routine dialogue in the production of psychological processes like repression. In this

72 Rhetoric and ideological dilemmas

theoretical perspective, he interconnects the use of spoken discourse with psychoanalytic concepts. He argues that since the focus of discursive psychologists is to examine what individuals socially do with emotions and other psychological states, they should treat psychoanalytic discourse "as a topic of investigation" (Billig, 1997: 142) rather than as a discourse that can reveal about other discourses. For example, they ought to study how people talk about repression and not state that the conversation was based upon repression. This is because there are social conventions and rules for the use of psychological language, like speaking about one's emotions. In other words, one's emotions, unconscious motives, are largely influenced by social and ideological factors as claimed by Bakhtin/ Volosinov (1994). The moot point, however, is that these psychoanalytic explanations are given in ordinary language, and everyday routine talk needs to be investigated for understanding psychological explanations that people use for themselves and the behaviour of others. Drawing on the techniques and tenets of conversation analysis, Billig further argues that the sequential organisation of talk shows its structural and orderly nature (Turnbull 2003) whereby meanings of particular sequences are sought through the meanings of previous sequences. Not only this, but the aim of conversation is harmony and mitigation of conflict, thus allowing the speakers to use indirectness and politeness strategies to convey their message without hurting the sentiments of others and escalating the conflict. For instance, they demand and order in indirect ways (Tsui 1989, 1998), they tone down their refusals and they often say things that are required as part of conversation, highlighting its normative structure. However, even then there is evidence for rudeness. Thus, one can say that people are motivated to engage in politeness, but there are "temptations to act directly in ways which rudely throw off the complex restraints" (Billig, 1997: 149) of normative talk.

Billig argues that this dual nature of dialogic conversation is found in the training of children; when adults teach children to speak politely, they are also teaching them to avoid impoliteness. In other words, children are being instructed to repress discursive impoliteness in favour of discursive politeness. This indicates the possibility of a dialogic unconscious whereby dialogic repression routinely takes place. "Repression can be seen as dialogic, for dialogue involves both the creation of desires and their routine repression" (Billig, 2004: 100). Speakers might repress what is socially and morally unacceptable in conversation that can reflect a "general culture of ideology" (Ibid.), and such patterns of conversation vary in families and societies, depending on what is acceptable in their culture. Thus, an analysis of discursive repression is in effect an analysis of ideology. Billig explains this through the famous case study of Dora, who was brought to Freud by her father for a cure for hysteria. On examination, Freud found that Dora's father was in a prolonged relationship with the wife of a man named Herr K., who had made several overt and covert attempts to pursue Dora romantically and sexually, giving her gifts, flowers and once even entering her room when she slept. When Dora informed her father about this situation, he refused to believe her and brought her to Freud for treatment of hysteria. In talking to Dora, Freud found evidence of repression of her feelings for Herr K. More importantly, Billig suggests that repression was being produced not just by Dora but by her entire family, wherein they chose to ignore the actual implications of Herr K.'s routine visits, treating them as a habit or a joke because such an arrangement was convenient to the family, especially Dora's father who wished to continue his affair. Repression was an overt social activity where normal conversation about Herr K. and Dora "functioned to repress other, more obvious interpretations" (Billig, 1997: 154). Thus, an examination of repression requires exploring the structure of everyday conversation and its contexts.

Summing up

Billig's works represent an unconventional yet unique strand of discursive psychology in many ways. Unlike the earlier writings by Edwards and Potter (1992), Potter and Wetherell (1987) and van Dijk (2009), Billig does not provide a step-by-step guide on analysis but a way of thinking, perceiving and understanding. His work is anti-cognitivist, yet there are no 'how to do it' procedures. His works have numerous illustrations from daily life, Greco-Roman antiquity and Jewish scriptures, and in this sense his writings can be viewed as an argumentation on arguing and thinking. Similar is the case with his engagement with ideology and dilemmas. Unlike the DAM model, it is thoroughly critical and non-methodological, yet highly useful for understanding the workings of ideology as constructed through conflicting views in everyday life. The subtle intersections of language, ideology and cognition provide a textured and insightful understanding of human behaviour, and in this broad sense it is similar to context models and Wetherell's approach. His argument for a more dynamic unconscious is in stark contrast to the traditional Freudian psychology, for it emphasises how the psyche operates through discourse and interaction, even though more research is needed for its sustained applicability. Overall, his works either comment on the importance of discourse or use its theories for a psychological understanding of the individual in personal, social or political spheres.

Suggested reading

Billig's *Ideology and Opinions* (1991) argues in favour of the study of ideology and contains analyses in rhetorical psychology. His main work, *Arguing and Thinking* (1987/1996), explains his approach, and his article on the dialogic unconscious (1997) is an accessible account of the nature of repression and its relation to discourse. There are several works on the working of ideological dilemmas and rhetorical thinking. Among them, Alan Radley and Michael Billig's (1996) analysis of accounts of health is interesting and useful. In addition, Billig's work on how people talk about the British royal family (1992) and Condor, Tileaga and Billig's (2013) writing on political rhetoric ably highlight the practice of rhetorical psychology.

6

PSYCHOSOCIAL STUDIES AND CRITICAL PSYCHOLOGY

Psychosocial studies

Discourse is relevant not just in linguistics and psychology, but also in interdisciplinary areas that seek to study the individual as a psychological and social being. These aspects are not correlated in the common sense but are viewed as intertwining cross currents that determine the subjectivity of individuals making their identities flexible, dynamic and seamless, as social norms and practices influence one's psychological states and vice versa. The social or the psychological dimension is not given primacy over the other, but the intimate connections between the two are explored, including intra-psychic forces at play, intersubjectivity in social interaction and the prevailing social structure (Redman 2016). The subject is viewed both as an agent for action and as an agent being acted upon, subjected to such diverse forces as race, class, gender, the unconscious, etc. (Frosh 2003). The discipline of psychosocial studies emerged not from mainstream psychology but from the intersections between psychoanalysis, discourse and cultural studies, mainly because psychologists viewed psychic states as internal and opaque to discursive visibility, a view opposed by Frosh and his colleagues. Discourse or language thus holds an essential space in psychosocial studies and will be discussed later.

Aims and objectives

The main aims and objectives of the approach (Frosh 2003) that focusses on a discursive yet critically grounded analysis can be outlined as follows. Psychosocial studies seek to explore the creation of the human subject through the operation of power. Subjects are not passively constructed as an effect of ideology but through interpersonal means, primarily language that both constrains and

Psychosocial studies and critical psychology **75**

enables them to exert control over their space. Individuals are agents who use power, are simultaneously operated upon and also show resistance in the Foucaldian sense (Foucault 1972, 1976, 1977, 1982). In most writings in this area, there is a focus on subjectivity as a result of the social being "psychically invested" and the psychological being "socially formed" (Frosh, 2003: 1559). Psychoanalytic concepts of desire, fantasy and narcissism highlight the eruptions in the objective social order in the way individuals experience the outside world inside them. Fantasy in particular (Žižek 1989, 1994, 2000) indicates people's emotional investments and their unconscious in understanding social issues of racism and prejudice. In addition, scholars in this area maintain a critical stance on social and psychological issues, particularly the latter; for psychology claims to have knowledge about human behaviour, hence its narratives and assumptions need to be critically examined.

Psychosocial studies advocate methodological and theoretical pluralism in an attempt to analyse the subject, drawing on psychoanalysis, feminism, phenomenology and critical theory to engage in interpretative, qualitative work as compared to traditional quantitative methods. Since one's experience is primarily expressed through language, an analysis of discourse assumes a central place to understand how individuals become subjects, how they are represented and marginalised and how power relations are bound with social practices. The need for constant examination of data (discourse) is relevant to show the applicability of different interpretative tools, concepts and strategies and also that language is not being given primacy over theoretical concepts. The scholars also show an interest in inter- or transdisciplinary research to further psychological research, ranging from literary studies (Andrews et al. 2000) to feminism (Segal 1999) and social constructionism (Frosh, Phoenix and Pattman 2002). Frosh's research, in consonance with the broader aims, is constructivist in nature, focussing on how discourse creates subject positions and the implications of choosing particular positions over others. The larger aim of such research is to intervene in the areas of psychotherapy, personal and social change by exploring wide-ranging topics such as gender, sexuality, religion, politics, racism, health, and psychology. Like other discursive approaches (van Dijk 2009), psychosocial studies too aim for self-reflexivity to examine people's emotional investments, why they do what they do and what they actually do when they purportedly claim to do something.

Masculinity studies

This section focusses on the way psychosocial studies explore notions of gender, especially masculinity studies. Drawing on psychoanalysis, Frosh (2002b) and Frosh, Phoenix and Pattman (2002, 2003) explain that gender roles are not strictly demarcated, and hegemonic codes produce counter-hegemonic discourses. The fluidity and complexity of gender can be understood in the writings of Freud and Lacan, who express the dilemmas and deep-rootedness of gender difference (Frosh 1994). Narratives of gender recreate and recount gender every

76 Psychosocial studies and critical psychology

time they are spoken but in new ways, creating "a series of provisional positions" (Frosh, 1994: 144). Frosh argues that if gender roles are constructed, then the idea of Imaginary is significant in experiencing and expressing the new visions of gender, linking it to Symbolic practices (Lacan 1996) "as a bridge to specific practices, that can challenge the way in which the Symbolic itself is organised" (Frosh, 1994: 143) for each retelling of gender can support, maintain or challenge the existing Symbolic order of social norms and conventions. His methodology thus seeks to unpack the various hegemonic and counter-hegemonic narratives of male gender and masculinity in non-clinical interviews among 11- to 14-year-old schoolboys and girls (more than 245) in London.

Frosh, Phoenix and Pattman (2002) found that young boys engaged in thoughtful, even poignant discussions with the interviewers in single-sex and mixed-sex interactions. Masculinity was constructed out of a network of complex social relations (gender, race, class, ethnicity and sexuality) and was not traditionally construed by the respondents (Connell 1987, 1995) but was built in terms of contrasts – hegemonic masculinity versus gay identity, with homophobia being a strong, recurring theme in the talk. Hegemonic masculinity dealt with 'hardness,' athleticism, sexual prowess, use of abuses, coolness and lack of academic achievement, while its counter-discourses were just the opposite. Talk was unconsciously structured; for instance, White masculinity was constructed discursively in tension with racist ideology and how the use of racism could be related to the "unconscious feelings of loss and anxiety about 'otherness'" (Frosh, Phoenix, and Pattman, 2002: 258). Also, masculinity was a performative, iterative struggle. Many of the respondents, even the 'hard' boys, struggled to construct a masculine identity, expressing their anxieties and vulnerabilities, and the discursive positions offered were highly polarised: hegemonic masculinity versus non-hegemonic behaviour which was considered abnormal. Most of the young boys were emotionally very perceptive. They expressed heterosexual desire for girls, lack of close emotional bonds with fathers and awareness of their problematic image, sometimes behaving delinquently to vent their anger at being labelled so. Moreover, young boys had a strong sense of morality, knowing that support, love and care were the basis of relationships. Social interventions were necessary in the way masculinity was construed. For example, arguing that football was a masculine game, natural to boys, created a problem for many who wished to explore other discursive positions. Thus, the social perceptions and upbringing of young people was at stake in this study of masculinity that showed examples of both masculine and non-masculine behaviour, conformist, disruptive and inventive.

Occasionally, the modes of alternative masculinity delineated not just counter-hegemonic spaces but also the fears and discomfort of the respondents. Two such studies are worth noting because they demonstrate empirically the use of psychoanalytic vocabulary for explaining the discourses of participants, as Frosh says, for understanding "each subject's personal investment in these discursive positions" (Frosh, Phoenix and Pattman, 2003: 52), their motivations for being who they are and its implications for gendering. One study involved interviews

Psychosocial studies and critical psychology **77**

with three school age children. First, there was the case of Oliver, who carved an identity for himself as someone who was not obsessed with football, stayed with the girls, was favoured by the teachers and was taunted by the boys for being girlish. However, it seemed that Oliver's non-macho image helped him to relieve the anxiety of sexual contact with girls, hence his choice for the non-hegemonic discursive position, even if it meant being bullied and teased by the macho boys. Another was the case of John, who swung between the discourses of homophobia and hardness. Lastly, there was Alan, who was openly mocked as being gay and whose discourse embodied bitter turmoil with his father, yet a strong sense of ethics and an idealised image of manhood as being imbued with care, support and feeling (Frosh, Phoenix and Pattman 2003).

The other study (Young and Frosh 2010) involved interviews with eight middle-class men from London, and the method of data collection, transcription and interpretation indicated concentric reflexivity – how language influenced the analyst from the initial stages of transcription itself. The respondent Brett underwent several contesting discursive positions, from aggressive masculinity to a gay identity, each with its own set of behavioural patterns. While Brett's masculinity was associated with fighting and drinking, his 'gay' phase was underscored by unconventionality of speech, clothing and behaviour which was apparent in his interview together with his piercings, jewellery and emotional expressions. However, what was striking is that despite his 'punk' non-conformist image, Brett also incorporated the traditional, caring, domesticated image of being responsible for his brother. His discourse, therefore, was posed between polarities of a traditional, masculine identity (with his brother) and a romantic, avant-garde non-hegemonic identity with others, voicing the fluidity and ambiguity of subjectivity, how it is constructed by psychic forces and vice versa, mapping the "unconscious, alongside social, process" (Young and Frosh, 2010: 512). Frosh's works are notable for highlighting how gender identity is formed through one's psyche and social practices, and his use of psychoanalytic concepts, unlike most of the approaches that deal with cognition and emotions, provides deep-rooted reasons for one's investments and choice of discursive positions. It shows a subject enmeshed, yet with the ability to choose socially, psychologically and ethically.

Narrative, psychoanalysis and discourse

Unlike social psychologists, Frosh advocates the use of psychoanalytic concepts in research, stating that Lacanian psychoanalysis offers ways of understanding human subjectivity as structured by cultural forces: "the subject is structured in and by discursive relations which are institutionalized in culture and manifested in linguistic practice, and through this are productive of human consciousness" (Frosh, Phoenix and Pattman, 2003: 41). Psychoanalysis is traditionally considered as giving primacy to internal psychic forces, as compared to language and thus the problem of understanding psychological concepts through language. However, the discursive or linguistic aspect is quite important for exploring the

78 Psychosocial studies and critical psychology

construction of subjectivity, since people convey their thoughts, feelings, beliefs and values through speech. Thus, the performative aspect of language cannot be ignored. In such a case, Frosh champions the use of psychoanalytic vocabulary as a link between cultural and discursive forces because Lacan emphasises that the unconscious is an effect of language and it is the language that creates our perceptions, giving structure to the outside world. The famous Lacanian example of a Mobius strip can be used here to explain how a person's identity is influenced by social norms, conventions and his/her psyche. In fact, Frosh and Emerson (2005) provide a detailed empirical analysis of the inadequacy of discourse analysis without being anchored in psychoanalytic explanations. Psychoanalysis provides insights about the choice of discursive positions by individuals, their intention, guilt, anxiety, etc., which cannot be achieved by just doing discourse analysis. Discourse can reveal the social forces of construction and the way in which an individual is constituted socially and psychologically, yet 'psychologising' is needed as compared to a plain textual analysis; "questions of motive, interest, investment and desire are relevant here . . . and psychoanalytic concepts and practices offer a powerful lexicon for the couching of such questions" (Frosh and Emerson, 2005: 322). In short, psychoanalysis offers a framework for examining "how individuals take up specific positions with regard to discourses" (Frosh and Emerson, 2005: 311) which, as Frosh informs us, a Foucauldian-inspired discourse analysis cannot adequately do. One possible reason could be that the latter is broadly a sociohistorical analysis that neglects the psychological dimension of how an individual becomes a subject and invests in particular discourses. Subjectivity cannot be fully explained without understanding how one's self is created from the other(s) and the deep-rooted role of psyche in the formation of the Self. In Lacanian terms, this means comprehending the Other as an individual or social force that 'extimate' (Žižek 1989); that is, both internal and external, present in one's wishes, memories and identifications, so much so that recognition of the Self is possible through the other. Frosh's notable contribution is to highlight this inextricable link between the Self and Other in interpersonal relations (Frosh 2002a) and one's choices both at the level of language and at the level of psychological investments. In one sense, then, Frosh's work is a novel attempt to re-present the psychosocial creature through language and operations of power.

However, the use of psychoanalytic vocabulary with discourse is not a simple, straightforward case of transplanting psychoanalytic concepts on the individual's discourse, since Lacan (1996) observed that words not only create one's world but also slip and fail to express what one feels; "language itself produces gaps and difference" (Frosh, 2007: 641), invoking the feeling that something more could have been spoken, as found in the analysis of an extract from A. S. Byatt's interview. Here, the signification and slippage of meanings in the text is not easy to pinpoint, and the narrative structure of the interview holds the text together, from disintegration. Therefore, Frosh's analytic methodology does not seek to provide a one-to-one correspondence between words and the psyche. With his experience as a psychotherapist in counselling victims of abuse, Frosh finds his

Psychosocial studies and critical psychology **79**

answer in critical narrative analysis. Narratives, according to him, are accounts where people not only tell stories but reveal themselves; and so narratives can help to analyse one's discourse, relations to power and psychical investments, viewing the subject not as an isolated, unidimensional entity but as a 'constructed psychosocial subject.' "In this way, agency may be placed in the foreground for analysis in relation to choices in, and accountability for, the discursive, performative distribution of subject positions, while at the same time interrogating the constitutive power of dominant discourses" (Emerson and Frosh, 2004: 131). The researchers argue that one's personal narratives can be better investigated by noticing the breaches between 'ideal and real' and 'self and society,' useful indicators of identity construction. In consonance with the multidisciplinary aims of psychosocial studies, Frosh advocates the use of feminism in studying gender (as found in his masculinity studies), and he draws heavily from James Paul Gee's (1991, 2005) notion of discourse analysis (idea units, lines, stanzas, strophes and parts), providing the following stages in critical narrative analysis for a thematic interpretation:

1   The interview process is viewed as a meaning-making enterprise constrained by both the interviewer's questions and directed by the respondent's answers, after which the raw text is transcribed for clues to make sense of the subject's positioning. The transcription is in terms of lines, marking strophes and anti-strophes (major themes in a text), unlike the CA transcription conventions followed by other analysts (Potter and Wetherell 1987; Edwards and Potter 1992) Attention is thus given to the organisation of the text as a narrative or speech, corresponding to Gee's idea unit.
2   The next stage deals with interpretation at the level of lines, in stanzas. Attention is given to discourse markers – syntactic, lexical and cohesive markers like pronouns, words and phrases – that reveal why particular connections are made by the speaker and their overall significance in the narrative. A valid question can be, do they reveal a disruption in the text or do they support the hegemonic discourses? This is the level of discourse, and I feel that several concepts from pragmatics such as presuppositions, deixis and speech acts can be usefully deployed here to understand the lines in greater detail.
3   The following stage includes the importance of the main plot or points from other material in the narrative. According to Frosh, the idea is to ask what is the use of this point, or how relevant is it for analysis. This is so because in personal narratives, speakers might have a tendency to speak a lot and digress from the main topic. It also helps to understand the speaker's overall psychological investment and social influences.
4   Deciphering the psychosocial subject(s) in the narrative, the shift in discursive positions and whether there are any patterns to the shifts, constitutes the next stage. This corresponds to the level of stanzas (topics under a particular theme) in Gee's perspective. Normally, the subject can be understood as the

80 Psychosocial studies and critical psychology

subject of the main clause, and if there is a change in the subject or their discourse, it can be an indicator of the "narratives constraining choices of possible identities" (Emerson and Frosh, 2004: 71). In other words, the points of view of the speaker show how they can be an agent of change and how they are subject to particular discourses.

5   Finally, the focus of the subject's speech and its link to the overall narrative is considered. Here, the word 'focus' is used by Gee and Frosh to mean textual material that is capitalised in the transcribed text as compared to other secondary material that appears in small letters. The focused material highlights what is important to the subject and in this sense constrains readings of the text and the overall narrative. It answers the question 'Why is this important?' and helps in thematic interpretation, employing concepts from psychoanalysis, feminism and other areas.

The thematic interpretation is dependent on the above-mentioned levels, and effort is made to find the psychological reasons for the subject's mental and emotional state and how he/she aligns to, resists or challenges power structures. Thus in one sense, the thematic interpretation arises from the textual level, requiring a re-reading of the text to fully understand the subject. This implies that the direction of analysis is reflexive (not linear) with a back and forth motion, where the text and themes are studied in conjunction. Frosh's use of discourse analysis is reminiscent of the writings of discourse analysts in linguistics. Though he does not make explicit use of concepts from pragmatics and discourse, his attention to language structure, words and cohesive markers highlights, that not just the social but even the psychological dimension can be understood to a large extent through one's discourse, albeit thematically.

Parker's critical psychology

Critical psychology is a theoretical and methodological perspective shared by a group of psychologists who are interested in studying the practices of psychology from a critical point of view. As Fox and Prilleltensky state, "we evaluate the theories and practices of psychology in terms of how they maintain an unjust and unsatisfying status quo. As we do so, we pay particular attention to the welfare of oppressed and vulnerable individuals and groups" (1997: 3). Critical psychologists view their work in contrast to mainstream psychology (the kind commonly taught in academia and practiced by scholars). Like CDA practitioners, a variety of views, strategies, terminologies and philosophical underpinnings are followed by critical psychologists; thus, critical psychology can be taken as an umbrella term for a conglomeration of research methodologies and practices that focus on issues of racism (Nayak 2014), homosexuality and gender (Kitzinger 1987, 1999; Walkerdine 1988, 1990), to name a few. It seeks to examine the following problems. Individualism and individual pursuits compound the problems of everyday living at the cost of compassion, care, sharing and community work,

Psychosocial studies and critical psychology **81**

creating difficulties in bringing people together. Moreover, economic and social inequalities create unequal distribution of resources and opportunities due to which the less advantaged groups are marginalised and oppressed. Also, psychologists unintentionally support individual-centred counselling practices, often using acceptable forms of scientific knowledge and normative practices which in turn supports the status quo, and many times those working in the critical tradition use the same practices and values to emancipate the oppressed groups. Thus, dilemmas need to be resolved by emphasising the welfare of the less privileged sections of society, by endorsing values that have transformative potential and committing to a political justice programme (Fox and Prilleltensky 1997). Critical psychology emphasises an exploration of the interdependence of discourses within specific regimes of power and knowledge and the possibility of multiple and non-normative identities within these regimes. For instance, transgenders present an interesting challenge to the binary of male-female, consisting of multiple positions, and a closer look at trans-knowledge and trans-communities can be a step towards understanding their complex heterogeneity (Martinez-Guzman, Montenegro, and Pujol 2014).

One of the chief critical psychologists is Ian Parker, whose brand of psychology delves into the social, moral and political implications of research. Parker (2007) broadly shares the above concerns, building on what critical psychology is and is not. Since it is interested in studying the dominant forms of psychology that have "saturated Western culture" (Parker, 2015a: 22), critical psychology has a strong methodological basis in post-structuralist theories which will be elaborated later. It offers a critical perspective that largely differs from the works of cognitive psychologists (Lakoff and Johnson 1980) and discursive psychologists (Edwards and Potter 1992), as it does not reformulate psychological states in terms of actions. Rather, it explores how different varieties of psychology are socially and historically constructed, containing powerful ideologies, and thus alternative models, as proposed by Parker, help to understand the naturalisation of mainstream psychology. Parker also argues that this kind of work highlights the politics in psychology that traditional psychologists do not wish to acknowledge. For instance, homosexuality was treated as a disease in the 'psychiatric Bible,' the *Diagnostic and Statistical Manual,* till the 1970s and was removed after a lot of protests from the LGBT community. Moreover, unlike the commonly held dichotomy between theory and practice, critical psychology is concerned with both, in exploring the proliferation of the psy-complex, a term that will be explained later. It employs a variety of methods (narrative, ethnographic, discursive) to fulfil its aims. Lastly, though it favours qualitative research, it also encourages quantitative studies that connect statistics to real-world happenings (Dorling and Simpson 1999).

In a more explicit critical stance, Parker (2015a) urges those working in the area to break free from three normative restrictions, namely, 'don't talk about yourself,' 'don't work with theory' and 'we should not address psychoanalysis.' As against the first rule, he argues that psychology would benefit from drawing

82 Psychosocial studies and critical psychology

links between biography, history, individual and society with the aim of making psychological research transnational, exploring different cultural contexts, not just Western ones. The second one pinpoints to the use of theory to understand the regimes of truth (Foucault 1972, 1982, 1994) that circulate in society and condition people. Critical of empiricist discourses that employ conversation analytic procedures (Edwards and Potter 1992; Antaki 1994), Parker (2017) broadly employs Foucault's discourse-power matrix (1972, 1977), Derrida's deconstruction (1976, 1978), Althusser's views on ideology (1971), feminist approaches and Lacan's use of language and the unconscious (1981, 1996) to explore how psychological subjects are constructed in Western culture to study the "disturbing and transformative effects in psychology" (Parker, 2015a: 19). According to him, these theoretical debates can be re-read, extended and modified in the light of contemporary events, and they are valuable for understanding a postmodern society (Parker 2017). More specifically, his take on discourse is largely Foucauldian, akin to what Žižek (1989) states that one cannot learn about the symptom by solely studying it but the way it came about to be, and for this purpose theory is very valuable. The third rule deals with the existence and importance of psychoanalysis in everyday culture and how it shapes our subjectivities through the discourses of films, magazines, therapy and advertisements; for example, the use of unconscious, fantasy, desire, repression, identification, etc., often denied by mainstream psychology, prompting Parker to quote Burman (2008) in calling psychoanalysis as the 'repressed other' of psychology.

Critical realism and postmodernism

Parker's critical stance and his use of post-structuralist theories, especially postmodernism, have given rise to debates between fellow psychologists and him. Parker argues that postmodernism is about "*deconstruction* and *dispersion*" (2015a: 31, emphasis original) of internal and external boundaries that trap the subject, wherein subjects are part of often competing and overlapping discourses, and its decentring of a unified, organic selfhood is attractive to psychologists who wish to break free from standardised, observable procedures and essentialist descriptions. Postmodernism is characterised by three narratives: suspicion of grand or meta-narratives, celebration of disorder and use of irony, pastiche and playfulness (Lyotard 1984). For psychologists, this means an understanding of individuals as part of a culture, not simply as experimental cases. The second narrative is characterised by an "intensification of a reflexive shift which accompanied the beginning of modernity" (Parker, 2015a: 34). This trend was exemplified by the reflexive activities of psychologists who were interested in exploring notions of truth, the dialectic between the Self and the Other and the constitution of identity crisis as examined in Frosh's psychosocial studies on gender. The last narrative gives psychologists an opportunity to break away from the binary representations of the world, such as absence-presence, design-chance and hierarchy-anarchy. However, postmodernism is not without contradictions; for instance, it

Psychosocial studies and critical psychology **83**

values equality of conversation among all yet also considers consensus as outdated. One of the main problems according to Parker is that "postmodernism makes a virtue of its ambiguity and uncertainty" (2015a: 40), combining all kinds of theoretical perspectives, and this creates confusion regarding what it actually is. Parker thus cautions against using the term postmodernism loosely, for it threatens the radical political agenda of psychology but prods one to understand forms of postmodernist rhetoric on truth, subjectivity and change through a dialectical process. He argues against the postmodernist use of relativism, amoralism and autonomy in favour of viewing subjectivity as a socially and historically located process.

Fred Newman and Lois Holzman argue against Parker's views, calling such views 'against against-ism' and stating that the differences between them are due to their different understanding of postmodernism (Newman and Holzman 2015). They object to Parker's argument for dialectical analysis as the cure for postmodernist reactionary excesses, explaining that for them, postmodernism is a "revolutionary activity – that playful, practical–critical, developmental performance" (Newman and Holzman, 2015: 55), and through it they hope to save modernism's self-reflexivity and revolutionariness from capitalists and academic Marxists, an oblique comment on Parker. They take issue with Parker's understanding of dialectics in the Marxist tradition, explaining their own as "a play without rules . . . of development, of becoming" (Newman and Holzman, 2015: 56), that can lose its usefulness but not its importance. However, they agree that although postmodernism can be a breeding ground for reactionary ideas, that cannot be seen as problematic; for postmodernist ideas have developed in all their complexity and are simply not a confused conglomeration of theoretical perspectives. They agree they risk celebrating lack of critical distance if it means getting back to the "authoritarian structure of the university and systematizing emergent developmental activity" (Newman and Holzman, 2015: 57). Parker retorts by arguing that Newman and Holzman's absence of critical distance highlights the postmodernist tendency to avoid political assessment of theories and practices within academia, maintaining a kind of mystification and mystery regarding the use of theory. He stands by his critique of postmodernism as a relativist, amoral practice, containing simplistic images of individual choice.

Another central debate in critical psychology is about relativism versus critical realism. Parker argues that relativism in psychology is helpful in explaining the truth claims and oppressive practices within the discipline, yet an absolutely relativist stance is not healthy for research, since it creates many problems. A relativist position creates an 'us' and 'them' in which neither side can win and both sides have their own perspectives. It also accuses critical psychologists of jumping to conclusions too soon, relativising the truth claims of the psychologist and in turn sabotaging the resistance-based political agenda. Relativists argue for perspectivism in which all claims are relevant and need to be articulated, often obscuring the lens of power and ideological analysis that is helpful in condemning some stances as dangerous and wrong. Moreover, relativism claims to be an extreme

84 Psychosocial studies and critical psychology

position by considering all points of view, but in fact it presents common pleas for tolerance and diversity. By contrast, Parker favours the critical realist position that grounds human behaviour and speech in social practices but warns of its dangers. For instance, such a stance should not reaffirm the power of the psy-complex, undoing the critical analysis of psychological concepts. Also, it should not accept things discovered by "scientific psychologists" to "be true, fixed and immutable" (2015a: 75) rather, psychoanalysis should be viewed as much an ideological apparatus in Western culture as any other. A crucial point is to avoid the "quintessential academic position" (2015a: 78), where all truths are claimed to be established. In fact, if one probes more deeply, they find contradictions in the surface of the arguments and the underlying stakes, revealing, as Parker says, the ideological nature of relativism practiced by some discursive psychologists (Edwards and Potter 1992), for they reinforce dominant ideas of academic knowledge as "*separate* from the world and *independent* of moral-political activity" (2015a: 79, emphasis original).

Potter, Edwards and Ashmore (1999) respond to Parker's arguments in several ways. They criticise his use of "intellectual trajectory" (1999: 80) from Foucault to Derrida, Lacan to Althusser, which creates tensions and contradictions in his programme, since concepts like ideology, constructionism and power are formulated in varying ways that have to be specified. They refer to the 'Parker complex' as a "dense network of theories and arguments" (Ibid.) that separates the radical from the reactionary to regulate what critical psychologists should do. His stance on critical realism too is accused of preventing his brand of theory from mixing with actual sociological, political and historical work outside psychology, and from insulating it from empirical research and people's views and orientations. The writers take issue with Parker's view of relativism, arguing that they advocate a serious exploration of the polarities of relativism like the fact/values polarity or individual/social binary, and relativism for them is not a "celebration of Western culture" (1999: 81) contrary to Parker, who considers relativism to be a full-scale perspective, creating confusion between theorising, analysis and philosophical argument. Parker's work seems full of rhetorical tricks that create confusion, a quality he accuses the authors of; and given the fact that he has in his career promoted discourse analysis and discursive psychology, how does his present discomfort fit in with his earlier views? Potter, Edwards and Ashmore (1999) are also critical of Parker's stance of 'critical realism' in and against psychology, questioning whether it is coming from outside psychology and declaring that, if so, Parker would have to explain and ground his theoretical perspective, which itself is a troublesome mélange according to them. Thus, in their view, the Parker complex is not much about critical analysis but about "a reassertion of its power and sovereignty" (1999: 86), and a lively Marxist discussion should explain critical psychology's stand on empiricism, evidence, science and the contrast between empiricism and production of method textbooks, among other things. Parker in response (2015a) criticises their stance shifting from relativism to uncritical realism, questioning their stake in pointing out his inconsistencies and whether his writings are *of* psychology or *about* it. He argues that uncritical realism is 'safety curtain,' tantamount to textual empiricism; and to understand the paradoxes in their argument, one needs to embed them in a dialectical critique that pertains to issues of power inequality and ideology, and to view their arguments critically. These debates highlight differing epistemological positions, the ways in which psychologists view reality and can serve as helpful guides for researchers to ground their studies in a particular direction. Moreover, the debates highlight the need for poststructuralist and/or critical theory, albeit with caution.

Discourse analysis

Like the other psychologists discussed in previous chapters, Parker (1990a/2015) too employs discourse analysis in his approach. However, his understanding of discourse is Foucauldian, and he treats the text and its language as relevant for highlighting the operations of power and ideology. Textual language is not the focus but serves as the basis for understanding social relations. In this sense, Parker's use of discourse varies from CDA (Fairclough 1992), although both make use of Foucault's writings, since CDA emphasises language analysis to understand social reality, among other things. Drawing on Foucault, Parker defines discourse as a *"system of statements which constructs an object"* (2015a: 151, emphasis original), and he lays down a set of criteria for doing discourse analysis.

1   The words, images and analogies in discourse attain coherence only when discourse is grounded socially and historically, following Foucault's works. In fact, like Foucault, a discourse for him is a set of recurring statements about a particular topic. Parker (2015a) has an issue with the term 'interpretative repertoire' for it echoes behaviourism, and he cautions against the use of a limited range of terms and the use of grammatical constructions as found in discursive psychology (Potter and Wetherell 1987); this is countered by the latter in another article where they criticise Parker's tendency to reify discourses as objects, his notion of analysis as largely conceptual, neglecting text and talk and the iteration of the importance of 'interpretative repertoires' over 'discourse' (see Potter et al. 1990 for further details).
2   One does not find complete discourses but traces of it in texts that are put in linguistic form for interpretation. Thus, one needs to find discourses on a topic through textual language. Here, I think, emphasis on cohesive markers, sentence structure and vocabulary can be useful aids.
3   A discourse reflects its own voices and ways of speaking that have been commented upon and analysed. To understand how discourse treats itself as an object, one can explore the contradictions in it and how another person or text speaks of these contradictions. Here, reflexivity of the researcher is of utmost importance.
4   A discourse refers to other discourses, and this can be understood through the concept of intertextuality, how discursive chains are formed by reference

86 Psychosocial studies and critical psychology

or allusion to other texts. A discourse is about representation of the object that is defined within discourses through intertextual links. The contradictions within a discourse open up questions regarding the other discourses that can be at work. Contradictions are also helpful in identifying "different ways in describing something" (Parker, 2015a: 156); for example, referring to refugees as asylum seekers or in terms of an invasion, deluge or flood (van Dijk 2008).

5 Discourses create subject positions (Althusser 1971), and an exploration of these can highlight the ideologies in a text. Attention should be given to the roles adopted by the speakers, what they say, how they say it, what their speaking rights are and in what ways the participants and analysts of discourse are positioned in relation to it. In India, for example, discourses on sexual diseases are not openly discussed, and doctors who specialise in this area have a particular manner of advertising their clinics, as doctors of 'secret diseases' (literal translation of the Hindi phrase *gupt rog*). The ways in which the doctor and the client are positioned in this discourse, their social roles and the manner in which information is advertised are some of the questions that can be investigated.

6 Discourses are historically situated, and it is the job of the analyst to examine the conditions of its emergence and construction. The analysis is both synchronic (at a particular point in time) and diachronic (historical) in Sausurrean terms (1915/1974). For example, the discourse on sexual diseases makes use of family, medical and social discourses that have to be examined to understand why and how such diseases are a taboo, not only in the present but also in the past.

7 An analysis of discourse should be an analysis of its auxiliary criteria too, namely, social institutions, power relations and ideological effects that are reproduced to maintain the status quo in society. Discursive practices implicate social institutions and their "material basis" (Parker, 2015a: 160); for instance, medical discourses and practices with regard to the discussion of sexual diseases. Discourses also perpetuate power relations; however, Parker warns us that the two do not entail each other because there are also discourses of resistance that oppose dominant discourses, and such resistance is often a part of oppressive discourses, creating a complex social structure that cannot be viewed in a reductionist manner. Furthermore, one cannot talk of empowerment of the oppressed classes if all discourses contain power. With regard to ideology, Parker does not believe like other Foucauldians that ideology is false consciousness and mystification. However, he believes that analysts should avoid the following trap: that all discourses are ideological and attempting to separate ideology from truth. Instead, ideology should be viewed as an analysis of relationships and effects in a discourse, or a matrix of discourses at a particular historical time period. Opposing viewpoints can indicate ideological clashes. For example, the theocentric, religious ideology

Psychosocial studies and critical psychology **87**

of Catholicism was at odds with the views of those who did not conform and many people were burnt alive on stakes, labelled as heretics. Parker (1999/2015) provides a critical analysis of an advertisement for a children's toothpaste brand marketed mainly in North America, using the above criteria, commenting on the interplay of the discourses of childcare, ecology, family, medicine, its inherent contradictions and ideological effects and how the advertisement perpetuates the relations of power in Western society. Among other things, the advertisement largely uses therapeutic discourse, drawing on psychological notions of development and rationality to produce human subjectivity at one level, and on another, to reflect on the broader psychological practices in the West.

Lacan and discourse

Parker argues for the use of Lacanian psychoanalysis in discourse (2005b) as "one of the most critical strands within 'critical psychology' precisely because it is not psychology at all" (2005b: 164), as Lacanian analysis requires a different conception of discourse, not the text and talk transcription followed by other analysts. Parker spells out his use of Lacanian concepts as reworking of Freudian theory in so far as it is grounded in language and not "hard-wired human psychology" (Parker, 2005b: 165). In addition, he views psychoanalytic subjectivity in Western society as socially and historically created and located, and as "materially effective" (Ibid.) in such a way that people use, and are used by, language. Reading Lacan means becoming involved in some kind of "interpretation and reframing" (Ibid.). It also means rewriting those comments of Lacan that can be useful for discourse analysis, and in this sense his work provides cues on how discourse analysis can be done drawing on Lacan's views. He provides several points for analysing a text.

The first among these points is that a Lacanian reading does not require attention to the formal, textual qualities, but it treats a text as a system of differences in the Sausurrean sense and pays attention to the differences, gaps and ruptures that disrupt a text to find "elements that *do not* make sense" (2005b: 168, emphasis original). Second, Lacan is of the view that there are certain *points de caption*, signifiers that anchor a text and explain its meaning retroactively. For example, in a text on madness, there can be certain words, phrases or images that help explain the meaning of the text. Third, signifiers determine the meanings in a text that are not absolute but provisional, describing relations of similarity and opposition in a text. It is also fruitful to view the discourse in a text in terms of the Lacanian registers – Imaginary, Symbolic and the Real – and to understand how the unconscious is constituted as the 'discourse of the Other,' that is, the voices and discourses that speak through the subject. Analysis of what is unconscious to the subject lies in noticing the gaps and holes, knowing that what is said at "any moment presupposes that something else cannot or will not be said"

88 Psychosocial studies and critical psychology

(2005b: 171). The unconscious is thus what is said and unsaid at a given moment; it is both intimate and exterior to the subject, therefore *extimate* (Lacan 1996).

Fourth, discourse analysis also demands the role of knowledge – what the Other wants from the subject (*Che vois*) (Žižek 1989), that is, knowledge of the structure of discourse and the position of the subject in it. An understanding of Lacan's four discourses (master, university, hysteric, analyst) is required to comprehend the relations between agency, truth, actions and the product. Fifth, attention should also be given to the positions afforded by language – what the subjects themselves speak and the activity of speaking as such, referred to as the division between *statement* and *enunciation*. Sixth, in Lacanian discourse analysis, instead of focussing on what is happening in a text, it is better to look for deadlocks – the disagreements and people's stakes in them, producing an inverted kind of a reading. For example, the difference in masculine and feminine speech genres and an analysis of that structural difference is tantamount to an analysis of the Real (in accordance with the Lacanian principle that there is no sexual relationship). Lastly, the aim of interpretation is not to unravel meanings, assuming that one understands it, like the child identifies with his mirror image (Imaginary function), but to disrupt the text so that "its functions become clearer" (2005b: 177) even for us. The idea is not to place oneself in the position of knowledge, relying on master signifiers, but to recognise, interpret and in turn transform what they are analysing. Thus. the aim for Parker is simultaneously ethical and political, providing an awareness of how one's identity is structured in a matrix of interpersonal relations with the hope that awareness can lead to change.

Summing up

This chapter explores the use of discourse in two kinds of psychosocial research. The meaning of discourse is modified and extended in the works of Frosh and Parker. Frosh's approach makes explicit use of Gee's notion of discourse, coming closest to a linguistic discourse analysis out of all the theorists discussed till now. In contrast, Parker's understanding is more Foucauldian and Lacanian, and therefore relatively conceptual and abstract. In fact, Parker makes use of two kinds of discursive research, one based on Foucault's well-laid out notions of power and discourse and the other teased out of Lacanian readings; yet in each case language is not the primary focus, unlike CDA theorists. While both psychologists rely on a conglomeration of critical theories, Frosh's main strand of research focusses on gender, particularly masculinity, whereas Parker's work deals more with a critical analysis of psychology through texts and discursive practices. Parker's brand of research thus has a critical, moral agenda, speaking for the oppressed, which is in stark contrast to the relativist stance of discursive psychologists like Edwards and Potter. Frosh's stance also involves an exploration of the operations of power and psyche, employing methodological pluralism like Parker, yet the latter's writings draw more heavily from the Marxist tradition.

Theorist	Van Dijk	Koller and Hart	Edwards and Potter	Potter and Wetherell	Billig	Frosh	Parker
Perspective	Constructivist and critical	Constructivist and critical	Constructivist and anti-cognitivist	Constructivist, anti-cognitivist and critical	Constructivist, anti-cognitivist and critical	Constructivist and critical	Constructivist and critical
Understanding of discourse and psychology	Language as social practice, focus on language structures and social cognition (social beliefs, emotions, attitudes) to unravel power asymmetry and ideologies	Focus on language and cognition (metaphors, scripts, framing and identification strategies) to investigate ideology and power relations	Action-oriented, interaction depicts versions of reality, use of emotions and construction of memory and accountability	Action-oriented, use of interpretative repertoires for critical analysis of social issues	Action-oriented, dialogic nature of discourse and dilemmatic/argumentative nature of human thought	Focus on narratives and psychoanalytic concepts to understand how subjects are created socially and psychologically	Foucauldian and Lacanian understanding of discourse to highlight the psy-complex and voices of the marginalised

90 Psychosocial studies and critical psychology

Both researchers advocate reflexivity in research, but while Frosh advocates the use of narratives and empirical studies, Parker's analysis is more textual, focussing on the psy-complex. Both of them make ample use of psychoanalytic vocabulary and its relevance in exploring human subjectivity in the larger matrix of the social, psychological and discursive; yet here, too, they differ. Frosh's writings indicate a preoccupation with psychoanalysis at the thematic, interpretative level to investigate people's lives, while Parker critiques all forms of psychology, textual and social practices that perpetuate the vested interests of the elite in society. A brief comparative summary of all the major theorists is given below in the table, highlighting their differing perspectives.

Suggested reading

Frosh's (2003) article on psychosocial studies is an accessible introduction to the area. Frosh, Phoenix and Pattman's article (2003) highlights their approach to qualitative research, using discourse and psychoanalysis. For a more detailed understanding of discourse analysis in psychosocial studies, see Emerson and Frosh (2004). In addition, Redman's (2016) article clears conceptual confusions regarding psychosocial studies. An excellent introduction to critical psychology is the edited volume by Fox and Prilleltensky (1997) that contains articles by different critical psychologists. So is the handbook of critical psychology by Parker (2015b). Lucid introductions to Parker's perspective are his articles on critical psychology (2007) and his use of discourse (1990a/2015).

7

ANALYSIS

This chapter presents brief analyses employing concepts from the various approaches discussed earlier. A full-fledged analysis based on a particular approach requires examination of large amounts of data; however, due to space constraints, the analyses presented here are not exhaustive but brief and suggestive in the sense that they point out how concepts can be practically utilised in one's area of research. Mostly texts from print media and interview transcripts have been taken in tune with the objectives and aims of the approaches, especially their emphasis on spontaneous talk or natural data. Although many of the psychological approaches discussed so far do not yet explicitly use discursive and pragmatic tools, I employ some of the tools, wherever possible, to provide insights about the texts. Also, an eclectic approach has been advocated in some cases to highlight how concepts from different approaches can suitably explain the meanings of texts.

Interpretative repertoires

Potter and Wetherell (1987) explain repertoires as the use of particular words and phrases, stylistically and grammatically, that help to define the actions and cognition of writers or speakers. They are defined by the use of particular lexical and sentential units that broadly reflect a theme; for example, the various repertoires in racist discourse that reflect the variation in the speech of speakers. Rosalind Gill (2009) shows that repertoires are common in media texts, particularly women's magazines. Although interpretative repertoires are found across large amounts of data, here I will briefly discuss the repertoire of skincare as found in women's magazines, to highlight the way in which repertoires can be identified and linked to social practices and trends at the macro-level. The skincare repertoire is reflective of the feminine practices encouraged by the magazine to

92 Analysis

augment their sales, intertwining the ideologies of femininity with consumerism (Coward 1984; Smith 1993; Talbot 1995; Sharma 2018). I will focus primarily on the language that creates this repertoire.

> Keep your skin moisturised, glowing, and even fight off infections
> *(12 March 2018, Femina)*

> Homemade face masks for healthy glowing skin
> *(11 May 2017, Femina)*

> Pomegranate is effective in treating dull and dry skin
> *(2 March 2018, Femina)*

> Exfoliation is a process that not only helps remove dead skin, blackheads and whiteheads, but also smoothens your skin texture
> *(31 January 2018, Femina)*

> The universal skin dream: having a complexion that looks healthy, clear and glowy, with and without makeup
> *(4 September 2017, Cosmopolitan)*

> Sprinkle your salad with olive oil and toss in some avocados and nuts
> *(18 August 2003, Cosmopolitan)*

> Yes, black tea has a miraculous effect on our hair and skin because of its antioxidants . . .
> *(17 January 2018, Women's Era)*

> Water keeps your skin hydrated. Also, to increase the fluid consumption, you can have juices of fresh fruits
> *(4 July 2017, Women's Era)*

Skincare is promoted through a gamut of products and practices: the use of oils, face-masks, eating particular foods, drinking plenty of water, etc. The magazine articles are accompanied by colourful visuals and, in many cases, step-by-step instructions of how to apply the products advertised. Several magazines inform their readers about the use of essential oils that are used for various purposes. The speech acts of informing, advising and suggesting constitute the repertoire of skincare, since consumerist trends treat the reader as the potential buyer and therefore as more powerful; hence the writer cannot use more direct speech acts like ordering. The language contains a mix of formal (scientific and technical) and informal (homely) lexis such as 'hydrated,' 'antioxidants,' 'exfoliate,' 'blackheads,' 'whiteheads' and 'pomegranate,' 'avocados,' 'fresh fruits' and 'black tea.' The hybridity of genres makes the writing accessible and lends credibility to the information given. For instance, the definition of exfoliation performs the same purpose. Often, evaluative words (Fairclough 2003) are used

Analysis **93**

to attract the reader's attention, and sometimes there can be lexical contrasts to induce fear and increase sales: 'healthy,' 'glowing,' 'miraculous,' 'moisturised,' 'dull' and 'dry.' The word 'universal' is a sweeping generalisation, similar to an extreme case formulation for it develops the argument for a universal situation, namely, a problem-free skin, and therefore serves as an eye-catching term. The use of the pronoun 'you' creates a sense of belongingness, inviting the reader to become part of a community that is interested in their welfare. Most of the advice is repetitive, designed to impress the reader to pay heed to one or more issues described in the magazine. Ideologically, the advice serves to persuade the readers to adopt feminine practices to change themselves because of dissatisfaction with their body, and the self-care practices that the magazines advocate is similar to what Foucault terms as 'technologies of the self' (1994). Magazine repertoires create normalisation (Potter 1996), implicitly stating what is normative for women and what society considers acceptable, and therefore they can be powerful indicators of ideology.

Interpretative repertoires can also be found in interview transcripts. Although discursive psychologists (Edwards and Potter 1992) prefer naturally occurring data, Speer (2002) argues that interviews too can be a part of research, as they consist of the talk of real people and their views on social situations. An extract is presented below, from a particular respondent (here named Alka) that shows her stance on feminine behaviour. It is part of an earlier project where data was collected from ten married and unmarried women to know their views on femininity and the ways in which they tried to be feminine (Sharma 2018). According to the principles of discursive psychology, the script has been transcribed using conventions of conversation analysis (Have 2007). The words in Hindi in the transcript have been translated below.

> (.) actually: during college days I had no defined sense of fashion <I used to dress like a BOHEMIAN> at particular times you know and <people used to take> those fashionable lessons from me at times like I was very fond of blue eyeliner so >that was my trendsetter during my college days< but uh call it a comfort zone or anything >I was more comfortable wearing a pair of jeans and loose tee shirt than going to a college< in a churidar or kurti so uh I avoide:d looking you know girlish WEAK >ki bangles pehen rakha hai rings hain yeh hai who hai baal baar baar manage kar rahi hain* so no you know< my focus was that I'm there for three hours just to study and score good marks so that was MY CALL that you know my hair has to be tied up properly and just for the sake not to look you know very boring or pale or monotonous I used to put >eyeliner or kajal at times but yes most of the times my dresses were quite< uh (.) I don't know uh (hmm) loose casual bohemian in fashion
>
> *that someone has worn bangles, has rings, this–that, managing their hair again and again

94 Analysis

Wetherell (1998) is of the view that interpretative repertoires can show the various subject positions of the respondents and can be studied ideologically too, for deeper insights about discursive talk. Here, two repertoires can be deduced, unconventional femininity and traditional femininity, and each of these corresponds to the two subject positions of the speaker: heroic and conventional. Alka voices the repertoire of unconventional femininity in her narrative description of how she used to dress for college. In the initial lines she sets up a contrast between her lack of fashion sense, and yet being a trendsetter. The emphasis on the words 'bohemian' (repeated twice), 'loose' and 'casual' and 'no defined sense of fashion' is the key, for Alka articulates her difference from normative femininity using those words. The words 'trendsetter,' 'people' and 'fashion lesson' construct her heroic subject position; someone who is followed and admired by others. In contrast to this position, Alka creates an imaginary subject position (conventional femininity), simultaneously distancing herself from the latter which she describes as the practice of wearing traditional Indian clothes (kurta-churidar), wearing bangles and rings and repeatedly managing the hair, and she asserts that women who are weak, girlish and sloppy overemphasise adornment. Her heroic subject position is closely aligned with the repertoire of academic achievement (scoring good marks, studying) because of which she ties her hair. This repertoire corresponds to her heroic subject position of being an achiever and a leader. An implicit contrast is set between girls who tie their hair and those who don't, presupposing that those who do are very serious about academics and vice versa. However, Alka's relationship with femininity is not straightforward, as she uses a blue eyeliner or kajal to avoid looking 'pale,' 'boring' and 'monotonous.' These evaluative words show that she does not strictly align herself with unconventional femininity because that would mean going against fashion trends and practices including the use of makeup. Her use of cosmetics, to add colour, highlights that she distances herself from conventional femininity to a large extent yet is not totally free of its clutches, imbibing and following it in some form. Thus, one can say that identification with femininity is blurred yet present. This extract presents a clear, vivid description of a clash between the traditional and modern aspects of femininity and even shows that variability can be found in the response of a single subject, that is, a person can have more than one attitude towards a social practice.

DAM model, argumentation and dilemmas

Given below is an analysis of an interview with a person (here, named Sarita) who had suffered a sudden heart attack. It is a narrative account of her ailment, particularly about the day of the illness. The analysis not only focusses on how her memory is constructed and the emotions employed but also on how accountability and blame is created through factual description. The aim is to understand how social action is performed through talk. Since discursive psychology (Edwards and Potter 1992) centres on how psychological concepts are recreated through talk, largely drawing on conversation analysis (Sacks, Schegloff and Jefferson 1974), the present analysis makes use of an interview, transcribed according to CA conventions.

> No, I'm not ILL as such I won't call myself ill but uh yes I have had a heart attack in uh June 2013 and ↑ ↓>that came as a surprise to me< because I had no uh >problem with my heart or any other indication earlier< . one fine day I >just got up in the morning< did all my routine work and uh it was about <9 9:15 in the morning> when I started feeling uneasy and uh I couldn't <place the problem exactly> what it was but yes I was feeling very uncomfortable and that discomfort increased . per <as the time passed> and for sometime I was >then I realised that I was sweating< very very heavily and uh then↓ . ↑then I couldn't BREATHE properly >I was having difficulty in breathing< and uh↑ ↓ there was no pain nothing at all it was just the discomfort and heavy sweating and uh it seemed >as if I have just had a bath< my clothes were all wet >absolutely drenched in sweat< and uh >then I called for the doctor my neighbour he came over< he's a doctor he he saw checked my BP it was little low because I had already taken my uh normally yes >I do have problem with my high blood pressure< so I take regular medication for that so I had >already taken that in the morning< my BP was very low so he said don't take your medicine uh for un tomorrow also ↑but that point of time I didn't know what it was exactly↑ nor could he place it but then he said >let's go take you to the doctor< but my discomfort was I didn't know what to do I couldn't even place >he kept on asking me what exactly are you feeling< I said I have no idea at all >I could barely speak< and uh then . of course then >he rushed me to the hospital and ↓my brother had also come they rushed me to the hospital< we went to the medical college and↓

The vivid description (mentioning the time of the year) provides details about her emotions, thoughts and memory regarding the serious incident. The fact that the account begins with negation – 'no, not ill as such' – and that too an emphatic one, yet a detailed description of the illness, underlines a contrast between what the patient feels now and what she felt earlier. In terms of rhetoric, the stance of the speaker is clear – it is a reconstruction of memory without any sense of helplessness in the present. This can be treated as a public account (Radley and Billig 1996), but because it contains personal/private details, the boundaries between the two are blurred, denoting that when people talk of their ailments, the discursive action is both private and public; they are conscious of what they ought to say, yet they reveal a lot. It is telling how psychological states are described in talk. Firstly, the respondent states that the attack 'came as a surprise' because there were no symptoms earlier ('no indication'), drawing on the normative assumption that most diseases are usually preceded by symptoms for long and therefore, in her case, the surprise highlights an ideological

96 Analysis

contrast. The actual description of the heart attack is developed more like a story where the respondent did her routine household work and then underwent a gamut of physical and psychological states – 'uneasy,' 'discomfort' and 'feeling uncomfortable.' The use of these words performs the function of not just developing the story but also constructing a body-emotion dualism where the body is 'invaded' by a foreign or particular state of being. Even her breathing difficulty (the emphasis and repetition of it) is constructed as a discovery, something she realised. The extreme case formulations 'very very heavily' and 'absolutely drenched in sweat' reinforce her uneasiness, and the physical act of sweating endorses the body–emotion dualism. The fact that she couldn't 'place the problem' removes all accountability of blame on her – if she only knew what she was undergoing, she would have done something, but this was not the case. She is an agent for she is the speaker of the narrative, but she cannot be held responsible for what is transpiring. One can say that her emotional state indicates her helplessness at handling the problem.

The argument about the BP medication too might seem like a contributive factor for the diagnosis and the way she explains and justifies it, provides details and displays her ignorance of her actual physical state. The entry of the doctor shows that he would know what is happening to her (a category entitlement); yet she negates this, maybe holding him responsible for not diagnosing the problem. He is constructed as equally ignorant as her, toning down his position and knowledge. His repetitive questioning, asking her what she was feeling and her lack of knowledge about it, points to many issues: her immense physical suffering, her sense of helplessness/cluelessness ('I didn't know what to do,' 'I could barely speak'), the doctor's inability to diagnose, hinting at his lack of expertise; and in one sense he is even held accountable for her state, but considering that he is a neighbour and his interest would be in her welfare, he is not blamed entirely. In fact, the disease is the culprit, creating confusion for both the doctor and the patient because of which she is rushed to the hospital.

The narrative is factual in providing minute details yet is based on both the participants' beliefs: Sarita's beliefs about the heart attack and her actual situation, and the doctor's implicit belief that lack of diagnosis requires urgent hospitalisation/ treatment. Consensus and corroboration can also be seen in the way they both cannot pinpoint the problem and how the family members (brother, etc.) and doctor agree on the line of management. An ideological dilemma is highlighted: even though the patient feels no pain and has not been ill, she suffers a heart attack, showing how common medical beliefs about illnesses (pain in the chest, arm or shoulder in case of a heart attack) are ingrained in the minds of patients, and how they react when their case is non-normative as is displayed below. An ideological contrast is also created between the seriousness of the problem and the modern medical treatment and facilities. The repetition of treatment and the emphasis on the words 'immediately' and 'fortunately' reinforce this aspect. The private world of the respondent becomes public as she talks about the marvels of medical intervention. The category entitlement of doctors having sound medical knowledge to save the lives of patients is clearly understood here. One can even say that the severity of the attack is mitigated by the emphasis on treatment (surgery, angioplasty, handling the arterial blockage) making the ending unproblematic and smooth.

↑>there of course it was just fortunate< I didn't know how serious it was or how slight it was but later on I was TOLD that yes it was a very massive attack and >I didn't know< what >normally I had heard that when you have a heart attack you have pain in your chest or in your arm or back or shoulder or whatever it is< but I had no pain whatsoever so it was >very difficult for me< to uh gauge that whether it was a heart attack or not >it could have been anything for me (hmm interviewer)< but uh when I reached there fortunately >the doctors were all put on alert they had already prepared with medication< and time less time was spent and I was given proper treatment immediately and I think I survived the attack

The dilemma of dealing with the reality of being a heart patient yet undergoing a successful operation continues the contrast between illness and science. Though the respondent begins with negation of illness at the present moment, ironically she describes her illness in great detail and indirectly her attitude towards coping with the past in the present. The repetition of technological progress, the extreme case formulation 'really advanced,' the idioms 'hale and hearty' and 'up and about' develop this together with the contrast between illness and good health, particularly the patient's views on it. It can indicate the respondent's praise for medical science and her coping with the reality post trauma. Also, the phrases 'no problem at all,' 'perfectly alright,' 'not curtailing . . . activities' and 'yes I had a heart attack' indicates the latter, because the patient does not hold the common belief that heart patients lead a restricted life; her opinion is contrary, veering towards optimism.

and the third the next day >that was the third day of the attack they discharged me< so I think that technology has and medical technology >has really advanced so that you go in for a with a severe attack and you come back hale and hearty and you are up and about< ↑and now I have no problem at all its just that once in a while I do realize that yes I had a heart attack but its not uh curtailing my activities or any other or giving rise to any other problem I am perfectly alright so >I don't even call myself a heart patient< yes of course when I want to put pressure on people I say yes I am a heart patient (both laugh) that's it

The arguments in these extracts broadly centre around ignorance and knowledge about the disease, agency to act versus non-agency, medical science and illness and trauma versus post-trauma life, and each of these highlight the thinking and attitude of the patient. Even though she has no control over the attack, she denies the reality of being a heart patient and curbing her daily activities of living. Her jibe about putting pressure on people to get her way indicates her need to be in control, in contrast to her earlier helplessness, and is in consonance with her optimism. Acknowledging the severity of the attack (she was told, she didn't realise it on her own) would make any patient depressed and demotivated, and thus her public account of the illness is replete with comments about her well-being. In terms of footing (Goffman 1981), since this is an interview recording and a first-person reportage, a patient would naturally highlight a positive and strong public image before the interviewer, and this could be one of the reasons for her optimism. She projects a divided and contrastive Self at different points in this personal narrative, each revealing her stance – someone who is weak, strong, ill and healthy – and her discursive action of reconstructing her memory, holding doctors accountable for their actions and discussing the dilemmas of health and illness, clearly favouring the former.

Media analysis

Another account from a media text clearly highlights how blame and account-ability is created through discursive action. This is a news report from *Hindustan Times* titled 'Wife Hammers Navy Staff to Death in Goa' (electronic version) dated 2 June 2019 about a wife being a victim of domestic violence and killing her husband in a fit of rage. The brief article is essentially a news reportage, about the killing, in the words of the deputy superintendent of police, Goa, India. The two sides of the story are briefly described: the husband's prolonged history of domestic violence and the wife's consequent actions. The category entitlement of the narrator (police officer) gives her the power to talk about the incident and also a sense of credulity to her words. The presentation of information by the narrator, though factual, attributes the blame on both the parties but more so on the husband. The sentences/phrases that demand greater attention are as follows:

> allegedly had a history of alcohol-fuelled domestic violence
>> broke the cooler
>> anger got better of her
>
> *(Hindustan Times, 2 June 2019)*

The husband and his actions are introduced by the use of sentences/phrases like he 'allegedly had a history of alcohol-fuelled domestic violence', he 'broke the cooler' and quarrelled with his wife on the night of his death indicating that his actions were long term, repetitive and violent. Through all these incidents, the narrator is attributing the blame on the husband for the actions of his wife and developing an image of him as a brutal assaulter, an abuser and the one who provoked his partner to take an extreme step. Thus in one sense, by stating the cause for the wife's actions and forming a cause-effect link, the woman's behaviour

Analysis **99**

is getting mitigated or toned down. The word 'allegedly' has been used in the report as a common media practice, because the information, especially the history of the domestic violence perpetuated by the husband, cannot be confirmed.

The wife's conduct, particularly the act of killing her spouse, is stated in a matter-of-fact manner, a kind of impersonal construction. She is someone who became enraged by the repetitive abuse and the phrase used for her is that her 'anger got better of her' and she slew him. This expression and the words 'hammered' and 'bludgeoned' are the salient words that attribute the responsibility of the killing to the wife, producing a violent image of her and the act she engaged in. Apart from this phrase, there is no other description of the crime. In fact, it is reported that there were 12–14 injuries on the husband's head betraying the gravity and brutality of the act but the narrator does not dwell on it in detail, except in a factual/impersonal manner. It seems as if the long-term abuse by her spouse justified her violent action. Moreover, a sympathetic image is created of her when she calls the neighbours for help, realising the gravity of her act, and she is later arrested plus her testimony recorded. This article shows that even though both the parties are blamed, yet by drawing a cause and effect link between the husband and wife's actions, the report holds the husband accountable as the main culprit and perpetrator, and the wife as the long-term sufferer. Thus, more word space is given to explaining the history rather than the actual killing. In this sense, even though the crime is committed by a woman yet the fact that she has been a perpetual victim of domestic violence far outweighs what she has done. Alternatively one can say that, as the narrator of the incident is a woman police officer she might have been enraged at the abuser's behaviour and sympathetic towards the victim.

Sociocognitive approach and rhetoric

> At what point shall we expect the approach of danger? By what means shall we fortify against it? Shall we expect some transatlantic military giant, to step the Ocean, and crush us at a blow? Never! All the armies of Europe, Asia and Africa combined, with all the treasure of the earth (our own excepted) in their military chest; with a Bonaparte for a commander, could not by force, take a drink from the Ohio, or make a track on the Blue Ridge, in a trial of a thousand years.
>
> At what point then is the approach of danger to be expected? I answer, if it ever reach us, it must spring up amongst us. It cannot come from abroad. If destruction be our lot, we must ourselves be its author and finisher. As a nation of freemen, we must live through all time, or die by suicide.

This is a brief extract from former American President Abraham Lincoln's speech in Illinois in 1838 on the "Perpetuation of Our Political Institutions" in which he argues against mob law taking over the spirit of democracy and its political structure. In terms of van Dijk's context model, the speech can be read as a persuasive document in the pragmatics of communication and political rhetoric.

100 Analysis

Moreover, it highlights the attitude, beliefs and emotions of the speaker, skilfully combining language analysis with the cognition of the speaker. The different modes of communication (written and spoken) are one of the first noticeable features of any interaction. Here, the speech is in the written form, yet when it was spoken, paralinguistic factors such as intonation, prosody, facial expressions and body language would have been important in conveying the message. The audience is the intended recipient hence the participant framework includes both, yet it is a monologue for only one person speaks. Intersubjectivity is assumed when the audience listens to the speaker. The setting of the speech is in 1838 before Lincoln became president, and the language analysis highlights many issues that the American people were facing at that time.

The topic of conversation is danger that is expressed through iterative questions which are answered by the speaker, a rhetorical strategy employed by several politicians. The microstructures of talk help understand the macrostructural themes of danger, law, order and mob anarchy. The temporal adverb 'at what point' and the inclusive pronoun 'we' set the tone of the talk, creating an affinity between the speaker and the audience. The contrast between 'danger' and 'fortify against it' constructs the problem and the argument of the speaker which is later answered. The use of the hypothetical enemy and the lexis for it ('transatlantic military giant,' 'crush us at a blow') develops the magnitude of the sociopolitical problem, simultaneously negating it. Its negation shows that the enemy is not external but lies within. The repetitive use of the modal plus pronoun 'shall we' denotes the firm beliefs of the speaker regarding the course of action, and by aligning himself with the people of America, Lincoln is able to speak more assertively with a sense of belongingness. The exclamatory single word 'never' and the next statement reinforce and expand his views. Figuratively, it is a series of hyperboles ('treasure of the earth,' 'take a drink from the Ohio' and 'make a track') that exaggerate the matter yet negate the force of an external conquest while asserting the power of the American people and the courage of its armed forces. Lincoln uses rhetorical language to confirm the supremacy of America and its independence declared in the late 1770s from the British. Even the name of the French ruler Bonaparte, who was considered invincible at one point in time, and the modal plus phrase 'could not by force take' are employed to reinforce American power. The hyperbole 'trial of thousand years' indicates the assumed repetitive but defeated attempts of the enemy to conquer. Till here the argument structure consists of question–and–answer pairs that are self-answered by the speaker, constructing the problem which is elaborated in the subsequent paragraph.

The next paragraph, too, begins with a question, but instead of providing a hypothetical answer, Lincoln gives the main answer, highlighting his beliefs. The explicit use of the phrase 'I answer' is simultaneously a speech act of declaring and asserting his views and answering the questions raised so far. The answer sets up an explicit ideological dilemma (Billig et al. 1988) protecting the American people from Americans themselves, denoting the themes of anarchy, lawlessness and mob law, examples of which are given by Lincoln in the rest of his speech like the hanging and robbing of common people from both White and Black races. The contrastive words 'author' and 'finisher' further reinforce this; Americans are the creators of the problem and they have to solve it. The repetitive denial of an outside enemy endorses Lincoln's views. The case is not of unanimous protection (as in the earlier war of independence) but of a divided country and people who have to grapple with internal political problems. Thus, the use of the phrase 'nation of freeman' entrusts responsibility on the people of America for the progress of the country. Again, the use of the hyperbole 'live through all time' and its contrast (suicidal death) not only upholds the integrity of the law and freedom of the nation, but implies a different kind of action from the government and the people. One can even say that Lincoln is implying sterner action from the government to deal with the issue. The hyperboles can serve as evaluative statements or sweeping generalisations that demonstrate the twin attitudes of the speaker, namely, anti-mobocracy and pro-action. Usually in political speeches, there is positive self-presentation and negative other presentation, creating a polarisation between Us and Them (van Dijk 2009); but here Lincoln creates a positive and negative self-presentation, contrasting the spirit of the American people and their foundational ideals of freedom, equality and liberty with the actions of the mob and its effect on the government, as he describes them later in the speech as:

> Whenever this effect shall be produced among us; whenever the vicious portion of population shall be permitted to gather in bands of hundreds and thousands, and burn churches, ravage and rob provision-stores, throw printing presses into rivers, shoot editors, and hang and burn obnoxious persons at pleasure, and with impunity; depend on it, this Government cannot last.

The lexis of burning churches, ravaging stores, throwing printing presses and shooting and hanging people creates the image of rebelliousness, disruption and anarchy, and even though the mob commits these actions against the evil or criminal-minded ('obnoxious persons'), taking the law into their hands is unconstitutional and illegal and reflects poor governance. Lincoln's anti-government and stern pro-action attitude too becomes visible here as he maintains that the government will perish. The repetitive use of the modal 'shall' denoting lawless activities is balanced by the categorical modality in the phrase 'cannot last' denoting the end of a government regime that permits lawlessness. Though Lincoln is talking about a culturally specific problem and the speech itself is set in a particular time period, it becomes 'glocal' because of the ideological themes of law and order, democracy, freedom around which dilemmas are constructed and explained. Lincoln simultaneously upholds and denounces the ideology of freedom; freedom from the enemy but an internal one, and freedom to act yet without constitutional rights. The ideology that serves the law and therefore the protection of the common people is supported. The social roles of Lincoln, the

102 Analysis

critic, the ineffective government and the people (as the mob and its victims) becomes apparent in this critique, and Lincoln emerges the dominant party for pointing lacuna in government actions and relying on law and popular opinion (vox populi; van Dijk 1991a, 2008a, 2008b) to subdue the mob spirit.

Psychosocial studies

The following extract is from an unmarried respondent (named B) as part of the larger project where data was collected from ten women regarding their views on femininity and the ways in which they tried to be feminine (Sharma 2018). The text has been transcribed in terms of strophes, stanzas and idea units or lines, corresponding to themes, topics and ideas, in descending order. The analysis can be done in two ways: firstly, according to the Labovian narrative structure; and secondly, the functional use of particular words and phrases in the text and their significance in the narrative, the latter as advocated by Gee (1991, 2005) and followed by Emerson and Frosh (2004). Some words in Hindi have been translated below.

> Strophe I
> Stanza I
> and how beautiful she is/ and you know rating her out of ten on that/ I don't think so that's valid/ FEMININITY is like you know how a female struggles/you know and outdoes haan* all these social elements uh around her/and makes a MARK this is what I have done at least uh I have done /
>
> Stanza II
> I know about myself/since like you know early TEEN AGE you know/ uh you know I saw friends around me like really BEAUTIFUL and uuhh/ unka* obviously that is how people use to JUDGE/ki haan* she's like you know centre of attraction/matlab* she is the one who OBVIOUSLY were more WELCOMED/you know rather than ME because/in them because wahi problem thi* you know LOOKS/that is how and femininity according to them they judged on that /
>
> Stanza III
> but I think sooner or later they PEOPLE REALIZE/once you make yourself, make a mark/and you know struggle against all odds/and uh prove yourself/that that is uh the time when people realize what femininity is all about/so you really don't need to speak/I think actions speak louder that words/so do rather PROVE yourself /
> *haan: yes; unka: their; ki haan: that yes; matlab: meaning to say; wahi problem thi: that was the same problem

The narrative's beginning orients the reader to the topic of femininity, then the complicating action about her life experiences constitute the middle, followed by the respondent's evaluation of the social situations and resolution, or how she dealt with social pressure. Frosh advocates the use of linguistic markers to understand the thematic concerns, relating them to social and psychological concepts, thus highlighting that individuals are constructed by the intersecting cross-currents of social norms and beliefs and psychological states. The use of the personal narrative has long been a part of feminist research (Smith 1993), for it lends easily to the articulation of women's issues or 'livid experiences' as Dorothy Smith (1993) calls them. The interview, too, is a meaning-making exercise where the interviewee is constrained by what the interviewer asks and the interviewer by the replies received. Though Emerson and Frosh suggest that the interview should be a dialogic process, more like a conversation where the written questions differ from the spoken form of talk, the data collected and presented here were from a slightly more structured interview. It, however, depicts not just the notion of femininity at the societal level, but negotiation and mediation at the individual level. The words beautiful and femininity are repeated several times to highlight the main theme of the text. The respondent criticises the social action of judging and rating women on a scale of one to ten, constructing a non-hegemonic discourse about femininity as achievement, how people 'struggle' against all 'odds' and make a mark for themselves. This tells us that the social perception of femininity as outward bodily appearance is the predominant or hegemonic discourse to which everyone does not subscribe; however, many internalise it as does the respondent. This introjection of social views occurs through significant others, often unconsciously, and the alignment or disjuncture from it presupposes that somewhere the participant knows what is socially acceptable. The respondent's emphasis on struggling against social norms or practices and making a mark is a non-bodily reference to academics or career opportunities (as she states later in her interview), and though on the surface it can be hailed as a transformative feminist move, there are crucial psychological reasons for adopting such a stance that are revealed later.

The second stanza of the extract tells a story from the respondent's early years, how she understood that some of her friends were more beautiful than her (that is implicit yet quite clear) and they were more appreciated and welcomed by others, underscoring the entrenched ideology of femininity as bodily beauty, something which is not acceptable to her. Degrading women to being just the body and not accepting them as individuals is indicative of body politics that is a well-researched topic in feminist studies (Harcourt 2009), and the notion of hegemonic femininity creates anxiety for the respondent, especially when she realises that she cannot match her friends in terms of outer beauty ('looks'); the comparison becomes apparent, as does her inner realisation of it. Therefore, her emotional investment and staunch belief in achievement and the struggle to 'prove yourself,' since she states later that people realise what she was. Her anxiety and inadequacy gives rise to her non-hegemonic or alternative discourse of femininity, and though it is a transformative voice, the reasons are psychological, stemming from a sense of inferiority, so to say. When she states that 'actions speak louder than words,' she is criticising those social practices and those people who probably stood against her but later realised her value and

104 Analysis

worth. This seems like a victorious women's struggle socially, but psychologically it can be interpreted as a women's non-conformity springing from a need for social acceptance; she performs actions to be accepted by others at a fundamental level, even though she does not believe in typical social norms. Hence, the desire for recognition and for inter-subjective acceptance from others propels her to excel which makes others realise her worth. The phrases 'people realise' and the iterative use of the word 'prove' indicate her inner struggle and personal desire. This brief analysis demonstrates that the psyche is inextricably bound with what one speaks and does socially; reading one without the other is tantamount to an incomplete picture, for individuals need to be understood as the Lacanian metaphor of the Mobius strip, thinking, feeling, acting simultaneously, in complex ways.

Discourse analysis in critical psychology

> When they are about to become teenagers, children become irritable, short-tempered and disagreeable.
>
> As they change your parenting techniques have to evolve too.
>
> Eat together – Keep the conversation light and friendly so they look forward to dinner with you.
>
> Make conscious effort not to curse, keep your phone away while driving, and practice the behaviours that you would want them to be careful about.
>
> As kids hit the preteen years, make an effort to find new ways to maintain physical contact.
>
> Talk to them, really listen to what they have to say, and to know their interests.
>
> Overprotectiveness and an authoritative parenting style stifle the child's creativity and growth.

The above statements have been taken from an article titled "Teenager Ahead" by Puja Gokarn that appears in the English magazine *Femina* (9 April 2018). The article deals with 'essential coping strategies,' advising parents on how to bring up teenage children. Here, I attempt to provide a discourse analysis of the content, focussing primarily on the aforesaid statements; however, the analysis is not exhaustive, but suggestive of the direction that can be taken if one wishes to draw on Parker's tenets of discourse analysis. Unlike some discursive psychologists (Billig 1991), Parker provides a step-by-step guide for analysis. According to Parker, words, analogies and images are socially and historically located, and traces of discourse can be found in textual language. Unlike discourse analysts in linguistics, Parker does not lay emphasis on the analysis of language but how language forms can highlight power relations, ideologies and the use of particular discourses and social institutions to understand the saturation of the psycomplex in society. This article essentially reveals the permeation of psychology in everyday life, specifically in parenting – the behaviour of the parent, the child and their emotions. It begins with a narrative of a parent in two different time

Analysis **105**

periods – their views about their parents as a child, and now their situation as parents themselves. It then presents tips on parenting techniques, interspersed with the opinions of psychologists and psychotherapists that lends credibility to what the article writer has to say.

The main object of knowledge is the child going on to become a teenager who is constructed as irritable, short-tempered, disagreeable and isolated, following behaviour patterns that are nonconformist. This information is presented by a child psychologist, and by virtue of the institutional authority invested in their profession and the institution of psychological practice, the behaviour of teenagers is presented as normative and commonplace, positioning the psychologist as a powerful expert on the issue. The teenager, who was initially a child and under the control of his/her parents, now becomes different, and the difference in behaviour requires attention. The construction of the teenager tilts the power balance in their favour as compared to the parent, as the latter needs 'coping strategies' on how to behave with their children. The focus is on how they need to 'evolve' in their parenting styles. The parent's narrative as someone seeking help reinforces their powerless subject position vis-à-vis the child, and each tip on what to do with one's children is a further endorsement of this construction.

The tips revolve around the following areas: eating together, practising what one preaches, ways of maintaining physical contact, developing common interests and parenting in a detached manner, and for each of these subtopics there are descriptions with caveats given by psychologists. Their opinions constitute the manner of speaking employed by the article writer to comment on social trends and practices in contemporary times. In addition, each tip furthers the construction of the two parties, perpetuating particular ideologies of friendship and democracy. For instance, parents are advised to eat one meal with their children wherein they keep the conversation 'light and friendly,' not talking about examinations, so that children are ready participants for such activities. The psychology of togetherness intermingles with the discourses of family, friendship and bonding over food as parents are advised not to sermonise at meal times. The same discourses can also be found in the next tip on the kinds of behaviour parents should be conscious of, knowing that their child will imitate them if their actions match their words: not abusing and using mobiles while driving. The discourse of mindfulness can be seen here, as parents are advised to watch their behaviour. The discourses of attachment, family work and emotional expression while that of friendship and detachment predominate the other tips as parents are instructed to give freedom to their children and simultaneously become more like friends than authoritative figures while talking and playing with them. A binary is constructed in the representation of the parent – commonly they behave in an authoritarian manner, but they should be more democratic – which is due to the teenager's demands for freedom or, consequent rebellious behaviour.

The article alludes to several other discourses, mostly as cautionary advice, creating intertextual links. For example, the discourse of education and examination with reference to meal-time conversations or the discourse of peers when

106 Analysis

publicly demonstrating your affection for your child, and media discourse that forms the backdrop for the use of modern-day parenting techniques. The latter, in fact, is one of the reasons for the emergence of the discourse of parenting in contemporary times. Unlike earlier times where the parent was the authority figure for the obedient child, the roles have changed, and therefore there is a requirement for a change in rearing practices. These intertextual discourses are, therefore, relevant in creating a comprehensive picture of parent–child relationships. Overall, the classification of teenagers, the coping mechanisms required by parents and the much-needed transformation from authority to democracy and friendship articulates the social changes prevalent in today's times in the urban Indian context (considering the magazine caters to the educated classes in cities). The article contains multi-voiced discourses that touch upon different issues. Although the article is on parenting, the suggestive advice given can put the article under the overall discourse of behavioural and psychological education of parents, highlighting the psychology of children and how to deal with them. It is presupposed that the act of reading would empower parents (a relatively powerless group in the face of teenage demands). At the same time, advising parents to abandon their old ways is a form of speaking against their old-fashioned techniques of power, empowering children in turn. Ably supported by the institutional voice of psychology experts, the article both constructs and transforms the images of the parent and the child, indicating their contradictions and the remedial measures for it.

8
CONCLUSION

There are many approaches across disciplines that attempt to bridge the gap between language and psychology. However, in this book, I have mainly discussed those discourse analysts who have used psychological concepts and those psychologists who have employed discourse in their writings. In the process the meaning of discourse has also undergone a change. In linguistics, the meaning of discourse has changed from a mere structural analysis to connected speech and writing that performs multiple functions and through which the operations of power and ideology are made visible, as seen in the works of van Dijk (1998, 2008a, 2009) and Koller (2004). Discursive psychologists have further modified the notion of discourse according to their research purposes. Edwards and Potter (1992), for example, treat discourse as action-oriented language for understanding how emotions operate through discourse; whereas Potter and Wetherell (1987) prefer to use the term interpretative repertoires to study psychological phenomena, focussing on repetitive use of stylistic and grammatical constructions in one's language. Billig (1991, 1996), in contrast, offers an indirect understanding of discourse as fundamentally dialogic, argumentative and cognitive, and through which psychoanalytic processes like repression are made possible. Those engaged in psychosocial research have also extended the meanings of discourse. Frosh's (2003; also Emerson and Frosh 2004) understanding is linguistic, narrative and thematic, while Parker's (2015a) is more conceptual, drawing on Foucault and Lacan. Thus, we find that discourse does not maintain a linear, restricted course, changing its persona and meaning according to the research aims, methodology and orientation of the theorist. An interesting point is that though most of the theorists do not confine themselves to the linguistic meaning of discourse, they directly and/or indirectly emphasise how textual language can provide strong indicators of inner psychological states, one's thinking and emotions.

108 Conclusion

The other related question concerns how discourse has been linked to psychology, and here we find that just as psychologists have used discourse in their own creative ways, discourse analysts too have drawn on and modified psychological concepts. For instance, van Dijk (2009, 2016) is interested in the working of social cognition (attitudes, beliefs and emotions) in interaction and writing. Koller (2004) critically investigates the pervasiveness of metaphors in our everyday social fabric, while Hart (2014) focusses on how meaning making is essentially a cognitive activity, using metaphors, schemas and framing strategies in discourse. It is important to note that discourse analysts rely on social and cognitive psychology and not on the mentalist paradigm in psycholinguistics, since their focus is on interaction and talk, and most of them are of the opinion that without the human, cognitive interface, discourse cannot be linked to society. In contrast, discursive psychologists view discourse as action to study the working of memory, attribution, emotions and even the complex process of thinking. Also, what is more interesting is how practising psychoanalysts have evolved their own approaches to investigate psychoanalytic phenomena such as desire, guilt, investment, fantasy, identification, etc., in interaction and their role in binding individuals to community and society. Such burgeoning research indicates not just an interdisciplinary interest, opening ways for new collaborations, but it also reinforces the common perception that individuals are created by the intertwining yet compelling forces of the social, the discursive and the psychological. Human subjectivity has to be explored in its complexity and totality, without being reduced to either of the aspects. One cannot exist without the other; however, the methodology deployed by each theorist varies.

This work also includes analysis using the concepts in each approach to indicate the manner in which research can be undertaken; however, the analysis is suggestive and not exhaustive. Attention to language structures, especially lexis, provides meaningful insights about a text. In addition, though an analysis focusses on a particular methodological framework, an eclectic approach can also be followed as long as the perspectives do not clash. For instance, Billig et al.'s (1988) concept of ideological dilemmas can be used with Edwards and Potter's DAM model (1992), since they broadly fall in the same area, as seen in the chapter on analysis. The texts to be examined can vary depending on the aim and orientation of the researcher and can be taken from a wide range of areas such as media, history, literature, sociology, politics, etc. Furthermore, concepts from the approaches discussed can be employed in hitherto-unrelated fields, but caution needs to be exercised in doing so, since an integration of concepts from different areas does not mean a mere transplanting of ideas but a focus on how interdisciplinarity can provide more penetrating insights on a topic. For example, concepts from discursive psychology can be fruitfully used with literary texts to understand the 'what' and 'why' of the actions of literary characters and how critics interpret such texts in their analysis. An attempt in this direction has been made by using and developing Billig's model of thought as argument with reference to Conrad's Heart of Darkness (Allington 2006). Similarly, problems can arise if we wish to integrate concepts from two differing areas, like psychoanalytic or psychological vocabulary to understand one's discourse. There cannot be a one-to-one, exact correspondence between one's language use and psyche; yet an overall psychological understanding of what one speaks is possible. Though answers to such questions are not easy, one can take cues from Frosh's two-level analysis by exploring a person's discourse at the textual and social levels, and by providing a thematic explanation of what is happening to the individual psychologically or psychoanalytically (Emerson and Frosh 2004; Sharma 2018). In such a case, the concepts and the area from which they have been taken have to be clearly defined to avoid confusion.

Another related issue is the scope of such studies. As mentioned in the first chapter, discourse analysis has an enormous ambit as seen in the areas in which it has been applied (both with and without psychology) like racism, identity studies, politics, gendering and homosexuality, health and media studies (see, among others, Wetherell, Taylor, and Yates 2001; Hart and Cap 2014; Wodak and Meyer 2016). It is interesting to mention a few studies that explore the interrelationships between discourse and psychology, underscoring that much fruitful research is happening in areas apart from the ones discussed in this work. For instance, a lot of research is available in cognitive stylistics (Semino and Culpeper 2002; Burke 2014), in particular, Culpeper's (2001) use of theories of social psychology, namely, attribution, schemas and impression formation, to examine characterisation in literary texts. Impression formation (Fiske and Taylor 1991) highlights how readers create impressions about characters in the reading process and how characters form impressions about each other, proving that reading is a dynamic cognitive process where the reader's attention is distributed unevenly according to their affect and perceptions. As stated earlier, Culpeper also draws from van Dijk's social cognition categories, like schema and attribution theories (Jones and Davis 1965; Kelley 1967) to explain how some aspects of the character's personality are inferred, among other things, through consistency and/ or deviation in behaviour and speech. How characters talk and behave in the absence and presence of others, what they say about themselves and others, what others say about them, what the narrator reveals about them through verbal and non-verbal cues and the lexis and paralinguistic features employed by them, all create a schematic construction of the character, enabling a textured and piecemeal integration of his/her personality. Culpeper's distinction lies in combining theories from stylistics (like foregrounding), social and cognitive psychology and pragmatics (like speech acts, implicature and conversation analysis) to provide detailed accounts of how characters are constructed, linguistically, behaviourally and psychologically, in the interaction between readers and literary texts.

A slightly different approach to the study of literary texts can be found in Norman Holland's use of reader-response theory (1975, 1998; Holland and Schwartz 1975) in creating and using the DEFT model that focusses on language, literature and psychoanalysis. In the 1970s Holland and his colleague Murray Schwartz encouraged students to respond to literature primarily through their emotions

110 Conclusion

and feelings, on the assumption that the student's use of emotions would highlight their identity and aspects of their personality; *"interpretation is a function of identity"* as Holland remarked (1975: 816, emphasis original). His model – defence, expectation, fantasy and transformation – explained how defence mechanisms were used by readers to construct pleasurable fantasies to transform unconscious content to the conscious level, and this happened through an active engagement in reading. In other words, attention to the language and phraseology of the text is a prerequisite for reading and can be an indicator of one's psyche. Although Holland's approach is literary and psychoanalytic, it has been useful for language users who wish to read literature in a second language and to understand social and psychological issues in those literary texts. The DEFT model serves as an entry point for simultaneous comprehension of the text and the identity of the reader through their gradual participation. Here, language becomes relevant in two ways: the words of the text and the responses of the participants, indicating that reading is as much a linguistic action as a psychological one (Grujicic-Alatriste 2013).

Recent studies by psychotherapists indicate the relatively overt use of language in psychotherapy sessions to extend and reformulate the meanings of the client in more useful ways (Peräkylä et al. 2008), particularly through conversation analysis. As Buchholz and Kächele state, "what psychoanalysis is begins to be defined in terms of what psychoanalysts do. To apply CA-methods to psychoanalysis endorses that line of thinking. CA contributes to precisely describe how it is done" (2013: 6). Practitioners focus on how the psychoanalytic conversation shapes up in the clinical setting by exploring the language of the analyst and the various mechanisms they use in their dialogic exchanges, such as the pauses, gaps, repairs, tag questions, preferred responses, lexis and sequential talk, since therapeutic conversation demands active participation from both sides. All behaviour, speech and non-verbal language (gestures, facial expressions) indicate the psyche of the speaker and are therefore part of the conversation, even the interpretation history, that is, how, what and why someone said something. This kind of language analysis reveals how talk is locally produced and socially managed to understand "clinical facts" (Buchholz and Kächele, 2013: 24), making the practice of psychoanalysis a dialogic exchange rather than an esoteric science shrouded in mystery, known by a few. Simultaneously, through the use of CA techniques, the discourse of the interlocutors gains prominence, as they construct their worldviews and beliefs and highlight their psyche in and through talk. In a similar vein, analysts have also discussed the use of speech acts in psychotherapy at the micro-level to understand macro-processes like transference and counter-transference and the power asymmetry between the doctor and the patient. Through detailed analysis, Schneider (2013) argues that linguistic tools and strategies (words, speech acts, utterances, intonation, sequences, etc.) are the primary indicators of the patient's psychodynamic processes, and the possibilities of meanings that arise between the therapist and patient talk can indicate one's emotions and actions, albeit retrospectively. This kind of original, interdisciplinary research is indicative of bridging the gap between language and discourse studies on one hand and, psychoanalysis on the other.

Lastly, another trend that is seen in combining discourse and cognitive studies is cognitive discourse analysis or CODA (Tenbrink 2015) that employs linguistic tools to study how people engage in cognitive processes like solving problems, giving directions, observing a scene, etc.; that is, activities of daily living. It uses the established research protocol of asking people to think aloud (speak) their thoughts and give retrospective reports of what they observed and perceived to comprehend their cognitive processing. The crucial aspect here is the use of discourse analytic tools such as turn sequences, turn constructional units, lexis and functional grammar (cohesive and deictic markers) to understand people's mental representations, not the decoding of sociopolitical agendas (van Dijk 2009). Thus, CODA uses discourse from a cognitive science perspective to examine people's linguistic choices in a particular communicative context; how discourse constrains and enables them to produce language and understand an event. The approach, drawing on cognitive linguistics, psycholinguistics and discourse analysis, makes use of rigorous procedures to establish and reinforce the use and ubiquity of language in cognition – thinking and representation. In view of the approaches discussed, the study of discourse and psychology is diverse, multi-layered and multi-dimensional, and it has benefitted from the interdisciplinary practices of the scholarly community interested in knowing how people speak and write, how they are socially constrained or enabled and what it tells us about their psyche.

WEBLINKS

www.youtube.com/watch?v=dAYzNNohlkY
Charles Davis's explanation of discourse analysis as part of coursework on qualitative research methods.

www.youtube.com/watch?v=EUeA0PEF_g4
Introduction to discourse analysis by the Educational Foundation and Research, University of North Dakota.

www.youtube.com/watch?v=F5rEy1lbvlw
Lecture series by Graham R. Gibbs on discourse analysis and discursive psychology.

www.qualityresearchinternational.com/methodology/RRW6pt5Discursive psychology.php
This is a brief introduction to areas in discourse analysis, especially discursive psychology.

www.discourses.org/
This is van Dijk's website, containing all his articles on the sociocognitive approach and critical discourse analysis.

http://oro.open.ac.uk/40676/2/40676.pdf
Open University Online's repository of articles on discourse and discursive psychology can be quite useful for those doing research in the area. This link is to an article by Stephanie Taylor on discursive psychology.

www.psychosocial-studies-association.org/
The association for psychosocial studies introduces the area, provides announcements on upcoming events and includes the journal archives.

Weblinks 113

https://discourseunit.com/
Founded by Burman and Parker, this website contains links to useful resources in critical psychology, the researchers in this area and the journal archives.

https://sites.google.com/view/criticalpsychology/home
This is a useful website that contains names of theorists, their seminal texts and information about journals.

These weblinks were accessed between January and March 2019.

BIBLIOGRAPHY

Allington, Daniel. "First Steps Towards a Rhetorical Psychology of Literary Interpretation." *Journal of Literary Semantics* 35.2 (2006): 123–144. Print.

Althusser, Louis. "Ideology and Ideological State Apparatuses." *Lenin and Philosophy and Other Essays.* London: New Left, 1971. 127–188. Print.

Andrews, Molly, et al., eds. *Lines of Narrative.* London: Routledge, 2000. Print.

Antaki, Charles. *Explaining and Arguing: The Social Organization of Accounts.* London: Sage, 1994. Print.

Ashmore, Malcolm. *The Reflexive Thesis: Writing Sociology of Scientific Knowledge.* Chicago: University of Chicago Press, 1989. Print.

Atkinson, Richard and Richard Shiffrin. "Human Memory: A Proposed System and Its Control Processes." *The Psychology of Learning and Motivation: Advances in Research and Theory.* Ed. K. W. Spence and J. T. Spence. Vol. 2. New York: Academic Press, 1968. Print.

Austin, John Langshaw. *How to Do Things with Words.* Oxford: Clarendon Press, 1962. Print.

Baker, Paul. "'Bad Wigs and Screaming Mimis': Using Corpus Assisted Techniques to Carry Out Critical Discourse Analysis of the Representation of Trans People in the British Press." *Contemporary Critical Discourse Studies.* Ed. Christopher Hart and Piotr Cap. London: Bloomsbury Academic, 2014. 211–236. Print.

Bakhtin, Mikhail Mikhailovich. "Language as Dialogic Interaction." 1986. *The Bakhtin Reader.* Ed. Pam Morris. Comp. Graham Roberts. London: Arnold, 1994. 48–61. Print.

Baron, Robert A. *Psychology.* New Delhi: Prentice Hall, 2001. Print.

Barthes, Roland. *Mythologies.* 1957. Trans. Annette Lavers. New York: Noonday Press, 1972. Print.

Bartlett, Frederic Charles. *Remembering: A Study in Experimental and Social Psychology.* Cambridge, UK: Cambridge University Press, 1932. Print.

Beaugrande, Robert-Alain de and Wolfgang U. Dressler. *Introduction to Text Linguistics.* London: Longman, 1981. (Original German Edition – Tubingen: Max Niemeyer Verlag). Print.

Bhatia, Vijay Kumar. *Analysing Genre: Language Use in Professional Settings.* London: Longman, 1993. Print.

Billig, Michael. *Arguing and Thinking: A Rhetorical Approach to Social Psychology*. Cambridge: Cambridge University Press, 1987. Print.

———. *Ideology and Opinions: Studies in Rhetorical Psychology*. London: Sage, 1991. Print.

———. *Talking about the Royal Family*. London: Sage, 1992. Print.

———. *Banal Nationalism*. London: Sage, 1995. Print.

———. *Arguing and Thinking: A Rhetorical Approach to Social Psychology*. 2nd ed. Cambridge: Cambridge University Press, 1996. Print.

———. "The Dialogic Unconscious: Psychoanalysis, Discursive Psychology and the Nature of Repression." *British Journal of Social Psychology* 36.0 (1997): 139–159. Print.

———. *Freudian Repression: Conversation Creating the Unconscious*. Cambridge: Cambridge University Press, 2004. Print.

———. "Discursive Psychology, Rhetoric and the Issue of Agency." *Semen: Revue de semio-linguistique des textes et discours* 27 (2009): np. Web Access: 11 May 2017. https://journals.openedition.org/semen/8930

Billig, Michael and Henri Tajfel. "Social Categorization and Similarity in Intergroup Behaviour." *European Journal of Social Psychology* 3.1 (1973): 27–52. Print.

Billig, Michael, et al. *Ideological Dilemmas: A Social Psychology of Everyday Thinking*. London: Sage, 1988. Print.

Blum-Kulka, Shoshana and Elite Olshtain. "Requests and Apologies: A Cross-Cultural Study of Speech Act Realization Patterns." *Applied Linguistics* 5.3 (1984): 196–213. Print.

Breeze, Ruth. "Critical Discourse Analysis and Its Critics." *Pragmatics* 21.4 (2011): 493–525. Print.

Brennan, Teresa. *The Transmission of Affect*. Ithaca, NY: Cornell University Press, 2004. Print.

Brown, Gillian and George Yule. *Discourse Analysis*. Cambridge: Cambridge University Press, 1983. Print.

Brown, Penelope and Stephen C. Levinson. *Politeness: Some Universals in Language Usage*. Cambridge: Cambridge University Press, 1987. Print.

Buchholz, Michael and Horst Kächele. "Conversation Analysis: A Powerful Tool for Psychoanalytic Practice and Psychotherapy Research." *Language and Psychoanalysis* 2.2 (2013): 4–30. Print.

Burke, Michael, ed. *The Routledge Handbook of Stylistics*. London: Routledge, 2014. Print.

Burleson, Brant R. "Attribution, Schemas and Causal Inference in Natural Conversation." *Contemporary Issues in Language and Discourse Processes*. Ed. Donald G. Ellis and William A. Donohue. Hillsdale, NJ: Lawrence Erlbaum, 1986. Print.

Burman, Erica. *Deconstructing Developmental Psychology*. 2nd ed. London: Routledge, 2008. Print.

Butterworth, George and Lesley Grover. "The Origins of Referential Communication in Human Infancy." *Thought Without Language*. Ed. Lawrence Weiskrantz. Oxford: Clarendon Press, 1988. 5–24. Print.

Cap, Piotr. *Legitimization in Political Discourse: A Cross-Disciplinary Perspective on the Modern US War Rhetoric*. Newcastle: Cambridge Scholars Press, 2006. Print.

———. "Expanding CDS Methodology by Cognitive-Pragmatic Tools: Proximization Theory and Public Space Discourses." *Contemporary Critical Discourse Studies*. Ed. Christopher Hart and Piotr Cap. London: Bloomsbury Academic, 2014. 189–210. Print.

Cattell, Raymond B. *The Scientific Analysis of Personality*. Chicago: Aldine, 1966. Print.

Charteris-Black, Jonathan. *Politicians and Rhetoric: The Persuasive Power of Metaphor*. Basingstoke, Hampshire: Palgrave Macmillan, 2011. Print.

116 Bibliography

Childs, Peter and Roger Fowler. *The Routledge Dictionary of Literary Terms. 1973.* Abingdon, Oxon: Routledge, 2006. Print.

Chilton, Paul. "Metaphor, Euphemism and Militarization of Language." *Current Research on Peace and Violence* 1.1 (1987): 7–19. Print.

Chomsky, Noam. "A Review of B. F. Skinner's Verbal Behaviour." *Language* 35 (1959): 26–58. Print.

Chouliaraki, Lilie and Norman Fairclough. *Discourse in Late Modernity: Rethinking Critical Discourse Analysis.* Edinburgh: Edinburgh University Press, 1999. Print.

Cicourel, Aaron. *Cognitive Sociology.* Harmondsworth: Penguin, 1973. Print.

Cody, Michael J. and Margaret L. McLaughlin. "Models for the Sequential Construction of Accounting Episodes: Situational and Interactional Constraints on Message Selection and Evaluation." *Sequence and Pattern in Communicative Behaviour.* Ed. Richard L. Street and Joseph N. Capella. London: Arnold, 1985. 50–69. Print.

Condor, Susan, Cristian Tileaga, and Michael Billig. "Political Rhetoric." *Oxford Handbook of Political Psychology.* Ed. Leonie Huddy, David O. Sears, and Jack S. Levy. Oxford: Oxford University Press, 2013. 262–300. Print.

Connell, Raewyn. *Gender and Power.* Sydney: Allen and Unwin, 1987. Print.

———. *Masculinities.* Cambridge: Polity Press, 1995. Print.

Coward, Rosalind. *Female Desire.* London: Paladin, 1984. Print.

Cruse, Alan. *Meaning in Language: An Introduction to Semantics and Pragmatics.* Oxford: Oxford University Press, 2000. Print.

Crystal, David. *The Cambridge Encyclopedia of Language.* Cambridge: Cambridge University Press, 1987. Print.

Culpeper, Jonathan. *Language and Characterisation: People in Plays and Other Texts.* London: Routledge, 2001. Print.

———. *Impoliteness: Using Language to Cause Offence.* Cambridge: Cambridge University Press, 2011. Print.

Dahrendorf, Ralf. *Homo Sociologicus.* London: Routledge and Kegan Paul, 1973. Print.

Demmen, Jane, et al. "A Computer-Assisted Study of the Use of Violence Metaphors for Cancer and End of Life by Patients, Family Carers and Health Professionals." *International Journal of Corpus Linguistics* 20.2 (2015): 205–231. Print.

Derrida, Jacques. *Of Grammatology.* Baltimore: Johns Hopkins University Press, 1976. Print.

———. *Writing and Difference.* London: Routledge and Kegan Paul, 1978. Print.

Descartes, René. *A Discourse on the Method of Correctly Conducting One's Reason and Seeking Truth in the Sciences. 1637.* Trans. Ian Maclean. Oxford: Oxford University Press, 2006. Print.

Dickerson, Paul. "It's Not Just Me Who's Saying This: The Deployment of Cited Others in Televised Political Discourse." *British Journal of Social Psychology* 36.0 (1997): 33–48. Print.

Discourse. Def. Oxford Dictionary. Web Access: 12 May 2017. https://en.oxforddictionaries.com/definition/discourse

Dorling, Danny and Stephen Simpson, eds. *Statistics in Society: The Arithmetic of Politics.* London: Arnold, 1999. Print.

Edwards, Derek. "Categories Are for Talking: On the Cognitive and Discursive Basis of Categorization." *Theory and Psychology* 1.4 (1991): 515–542. Print.

———. *Discourse and Cognition.* London: Sage, 1997. Print.

———. "Shared Knowledge as a Performative and Rhetorical Category." *Pragmatics in 1998: Selected Papers from the 6th International Pragmatics Conference.* Ed. Jef Verschueren. Vol. 2. Antwerp: International Pragmatics Association, 1999. 130–141. Print.

Bibliography 117

———. "Shared Knowledge as a Performative Category in Conversation." *Rivista di Psicololinguistica Applicata* 4.0 (2004): 41–53. Print.

———. "Discursive Psychology." *Handbook of Language and Social Interaction*. Ed. Kristine L. Fitch and Robert E. Sanders. Hillsdale, NJ: Lawrence Erlbaum, 2005. 257–273. Print.

———. "Intentionality and Mens Rea in Police Interrogations: The Production of Actions as Crime." *Intercultural Pragmatics* 5.2 (2008): 177–199. Print.

Edwards, Derek and Alessandra Fasulo. "'To Be Honest': Sequential Use of Honesty Phrases in Talk-in-Interaction." *Research on Language and Social Interaction* 39.0 (2006): 343–376. Print.

Edwards, Derek and Jonathan Potter. *Discursive Psychology*. London: Sage, 1992. Print.

———. "Language and Causation: A Discourse Analytical Approach to Description and Attribution." *Psychological Review* 100.1 (1993): 23–41. Print.

———. "Discursive Psychology." *How to Analyse Talk in Institutional Settings: A Casebook of Methods*. Ed. Alec McHoul and Mark Rapley. London and New York: Continuum International, 2001. 12–24. Print.

Emerson, Peter and Stephen Frosh. *Critical Narrative Analysis in Psychology*. Basingstoke, Hampshire: Palgrave Macmillan, 2004. Print.

Eysenck, Hans Jürgen. *The Structure of Human Personality*. New York: Wiley, 1953. Print.

Fairclough, Norman. *Language and Power*. Essex: Longman, 1989. Print.

———. *Discourse and Social Change*. Cambridge: Polity Press, 1992. Print.

———. "Critical Discourse Analysis and the Marketization of Public Discourse: The Universities." *Discourse and Society* 4.2 (1993): 133–168. Print.

———. *Media Discourse*. London: Hodder Education, 1995a. Print.

———. *Critical Discourse Analysis: The Critical Study of Language*. Harlow: Longman, 1995b. Print.

———. "A Reply to Henry Widdowson's 'Discourse Analysis: A Critical View'." *Language and Literature* 5.1 (1996): 49–56. Rept. in *Critical Discourse Analysis: Critical Concepts in Linguistics*. Ed. Michael Toolan. Vol. 3. London: Routledge, 2002. 148–155. Print.

———. *Analysing Discourse: Textual Analysis for Social Research*. Abingdon, Oxon: Routledge, 2003. Print.

Fairclough, Norman and Ruth Wodak. "Critical Discourse Analysis." *Discourse as Social Interaction*. Ed. Teun A. van Dijk. London: Sage, 1997. 258–284. Print.

Fauconnier, Gilles and Mark Turner. *The Way We Think: Conceptual Blending and the Mind's Hidden Complexities*. New York: Basic Books, 2002. Print.

Festinger, Leon. *A Theory of Cognitive Dissonance*. Stanford: Stanford University Press, 1957. Print.

Fiske, Susan T. and Shelley E. Taylor. *Social Cognition*. 2nd ed. New York: Addison-Wesley, 1991. Print.

Foucault, Michel. "The Subject and Power." *Critical Inquiry* 8.4 (1982): 777–795. Print.

———. *The History of Sexuality*. 1976. Vol. 1: An Introduction. Trans. Robert Hurley. New York: Penguin, 1990. Print.

———. "Technologies of the Self." *Ethics: Subjectivity and Truth*. New York: The New Press, 1994. 221–251. Print.

———. *Discipline and Punish: The Birth of the Prison*. 1977. Trans. Alan Sheridan. New York: Vintage, 1995. Print.

———. *Archeology of Knowledge*. 1972. Trans. A. M. Sheridan Smith. Rept. London: Routledge Classics, 2010. Print.

Fowler, Roger. *Linguistics and the Novel*. London: Methuen, 1977. Print.

118 Bibliography

———. *Language in the News: Discourse and Ideology in the Press.* London: Routledge, 1981. Print.

———. *Linguistic Criticism.* Oxford: Oxford University Press, 1986. Print.

Fowler, Roger, et al. *Language and Control.* London: Routledge and Kegan Paul, 1979. Print.

Fox, Dennis and Issac Prilleltensky, eds. *Critical Psychology: An Introduction.* London: Sage, 1997. Print.

Frosh, Stephen. *Sexual Difference, Masculinity and Psychoanalysis.* London: Routledge, 1994. Print.

———. "The Other." *American Imago* 59.0 (2002a): 389–407. Print.

———. *After Words: The Personal in Gender, Culture and Psychotherapy.* London: Palgrave Macmillan, 2002b. Print.

———. "Psychosocial Studies and Psychology? Is a Critical Approach Emerging?" *Human Relations* 56.0 (2003): 1547–1567. Print.

———. "Disintegrating Qualitative Research." *Theory and Psychology* 17.5 (2007): 635–653. Print.

Frosh, Stephen and Peter Emerson. "Interpretation and Over-Interpretation: Disputing the Meaning of Texts." *Qualitative Research* 5.3 (2005): 307–324. Print.

Frosh, Stephen, Ann Phoenix, and Rob Pattman. *Young Masculinities: Understanding Boys in Contemporary Culture.* New York: Palgrave Macmillan, 2002. Print.

———. "Taking a Stand: Using Psychoanalysis to Explore the Positioning of Subjects in Discourse." *British Journal of Social Psychology* 42.0 (2003): 39–53. Print.

Garfinkel, Harold. *Studies in Ethnomethodology.* Englewood Cliffs, NJ: Prentice Hall, 1967. Print.

Gee, James Paul. "A Linguistic Approach to Narrative." *Journal of Narrative and Life History* 1.1 (1991): 15–39. Print.

———. *An Introduction to Discourse Analysis: Theory and Method.* 2nd ed. Oxford: Routledge, 2005. Print.

Genette, Gerard. *Narrative Discourse: An Essay in Method.* 1972. Trans. Jane E. Lewin. New York: Cornell University Press, 1980. Print.

Gibbs, Raymond W. *The Poetics of Mind: Figurative Thought, Language and Understanding.* Cambridge: Cambridge University Press, 1994. Print.

Gilbert, Nigel and Michael Mulkay. "Contexts of Scientific Discourse: Social Accounting in Experimental Papers." *The Social Processes of Investigation.* Ed. Karin Knorr-Cetina, Roger Krohn and Richard Whitley. Dordrecht: Reidel, 1980. Print.

———. *Opening Pandora's Box: A Sociological Analysis of Scientists' Discourse.* Cambridge: Cambridge University Press, 1984. Print.

Gill, Rosalind. "Mediated Intimacy and Postfeminism: A Discourse Analytic Examination of Sex and Relationships Advice in a Woman's Magazine." *Discourse and Communication* 3.4 (2009): 345–369. Print.

Glapka, Ewa. *Reading Bridal Magazines from a Critical Discursive Perspective.* Basingstoke, Hampshire: Palgrave Macmillan, 2014. Print.

Goffman, Erving. *Gender Advertisements.* New York: Harper and Row, 1979. Print.

———. *Forms of Talk.* Philadelphia: University of Pennsylvania Press, 1981. Print.

Gramsci, Antonio. *Selections from the Prison Notebooks of Antonio Gramsci.* 1971. Ed. and Trans. Quintin Hoare and Geoffrey Nowell Smith. New York: International, 1996. Print.

Greimas, Algirdas Julien. *Structural Semantics: An Attempt at a Method.* Trans. Daniele McDowell, Ronald Schleifer and Alan Velie. Lincoln, NE: University of Nebraska Press, 1983. Print.

Grice, Herbert Paul. "Logic and Conversation." 1975. *Methods in Language and Social Interaction.* Ed. Ian Hutchby. Vol. 1. London: Sage, 2008. 24–40. Print.

Grujicic-Alatriste, Lubie. "Psychoanalytic Literary Criticism: Using Holland's DEFT Model as a Reader Response Tool in the Language Classroom." *Language and Psychoanalysis* 2.1 (2013): 20–49. Print.

Gumperz, John. "Introduction." *Directions in Sociolinguistics: The Ethnography of Communication.* Ed. John J. Gumperz and Dell Hymes. New York: Holt, 1972. 1–25. Print.

———. "On Interactional Sociolinguistic Method." *Talk, Work and Institutional Order.* Ed. Srikant Sarangi and Celia Roberts. Berlin: Mouton, 1999. 453–471. Print.

Hall, Kira and Mary Bucholtz, eds. *Gender Articulated: Language and the Socially Constructed Self.* New York: Routledge, 1995. Print.

Halliday, Michael Alexander Kirkwood. *An Introduction to Functional Grammar.* 1985. 2nd ed. London: Arnold, 1994. Print.

Halliday, Michael Alexander Kirkwood and Ruqaiya Hasan. *Cohesion in English.* English Language Series No. 9. London: Longman, 1976. Print.

Halliday, Michael Alexander Kirkwood and Christian Matthias Ingemar Martin Matthiessen. *Halliday's Introduction to Functional Grammar.* 4th ed. Abingdon, Oxon: Routledge, 2014. Print.

Halloran, Kieran O'. "Digital Argument Deconstruction: An Ethical Software-Assisted Critical Discourse Analysis for Highlighting Where Arguments Fall Apart." *Contemporary Critical Discourse Studies.* Ed. Christopher Hart and Piotr Cap. London: Bloomsbury Academic, 2014. 237–280. Print.

Harcourt, Wendy. *Body Politics in Development: Critical Debates in Gender and Development.* London: Zed Books, 2009. Print.

Harré, Rom. *Personal Being: A Theory for Individual Psychology.* Oxford: Blackwell Publishing, 1983. Print.

———. "Situational Rhetoric and Self-Presentation." *Language and Social Situations.* Ed. Joseph Forgas. New York: Springer-Verlag, 1985. Print.

Harré, Rom and W. Gerrod Parrott. *The Emotions: Social, Cultural and Biological Dimensions.* London: Sage, 1996. Print.

Harris, Zellig S. "Discourse Analysis." *Language* 28 (1952): 1–30. Print.

Hart, Christopher. "Critical Discourse Analysis and Metaphor: Towards a Theoretical Framework." *Critical Discourse Studies* 5.2 (2008): 91–106. Print.

———. *Critical Discourse Analysis and Cognitive Science: New Perspectives on Immigration Discourse.* Basingstoke, Hampshire: Palgrave Macmillan, 2010. Print.

———. "Construal Operations in Online Press Reports of Political Protests." *Contemporary Critical Discourse Studies.* Ed. Christopher Hart and Piotr Cap. London: Bloomsbury Academic, 2014. 167–188. Print.

Hart, Christopher and Piotr Cap, eds. "Introduction." *Contemporary Critical Discourse Studies.* London: Bloomsbury Academic, 2014. 1–15. Print.

Have, Paul ten. *Doing Conversation Analysis: A Practical Guide.* 1999. 2nd ed. London: Sage, 2007. Print.

Hogg, Michael A. and Graham M. Vaughan. *Social Psychology.* 8th ed. Harlow: Pearson Education, 2018. Print.

Holland, Norman. "Unity, Identity, Text, Self." *PMLA* 90.5 (1975): 813–822. Print.

———. "Reading and Identity." 1998. Web Access: 18 May 2017. http://users.clas.ufl.edu/nholland/rdgident.htm

Holland, Norman and Murray Schwartz. "The Delphi Seminar." *College English* 36.7 (1975): 789–800. Print.

120 Bibliography

Holmes, Janet and Miriam Meyerhoff. *The Handbook of Language and Gender*. Maiden, MA: Blackwell Publishing, 2003. Print.

Hurford, James R., Brendan Heasley, and Michael B. Smith. *Semantics: A Coursebook*. 1983. 2nd ed. Cambridge: Cambridge University Press, 2007. Print.

Hymes, Dell. "Models of the Interaction of Language and Social Life." *Directions in Sociolinguistics: The Ethnography of Communication*. Ed. John J. Gumperz and Dell Hymes. New York: Holt, 1972. 35–71. Print.

———. "Ways of Speaking." *Explorations in Ethnography of Speaking*. Ed. Richard Bauman and Joel Sherzer. London: Cambridge University Press, 1974. Print.

Jaworski, Adam and Nikolas Coupland, eds. "Introduction." *The Discourse Reader*. 2nd ed. Oxford: Routledge, 1999. 1–36. Print.

Jeffries, Lesley. *Textual Construction of the Female Body: A Critical Discourse Approach*. Basingstoke, Hampshire: Palgrave Macmillan, 2007. Print.

Johnstone, Barbara. *Discourse Analysis*. 2nd ed. Malden, MA: Wiley Blackwell, 2008. Print.

Jones, Edward E. and Keith E. Davis. "From Acts to Disposition: The Attribution Process in Person Perception." *Advances in Experimental Social Psychology*. Ed. Leonard Berkowitz. Vol. 2. New York: Academic Press, 1965. 219–266. Print.

Kelley, Harold H. "Attribution Theory in Social Psychology." *Nebraska Symposium on Motivation*. Ed. David Levine. Lincoln, NE: Nebraska University Press, 1967. 192–238. Print.

Kitzinger, Celia. *The Social Construction of Lesbianism*. London: Sage, 1987. Print.

———. "Lesbian and Gay Psychology: Is It Critical?" *Annual Review of Critical Psychology* 1.0 (1999): 50–66. Print.

Koller, Veronica. *Metaphor and Gender in Business Media Discourse: A Critical Cognitive Study*. Basingstoke, Hampshire: Palgrave Macmillan, 2004. Print.

———. "Designing Cognition: Visual Metaphor as a Design Feature in Business Magazines." *Information Design Journal + Document Design* 13.2 (2005): 136–150. Print.

———. "Applying Social Cognition Research to Critical Discourse Studies: The Case of Collective Identities." *Contemporary Critical Discourse Studies*. Ed. Christopher Hart and Piotr Cap. London: Bloomsbury Academic, 2014. 147–165. Print.

Kress, Gunther and Robert Hodge. *Language as Ideology*. London: Routledge, 1979. Print.

Labov, William. *The Social Stratification of English in New York City*. Washington, DC: Center for Applied Linguistics, 1966. Print.

———. *Language in the Inner City*. Philadelphia: University of Pennsylvania Press, 1972. Print.

Labov, William and David Fashel. *Therapeutic Discourse: Psychotherapy as Conversation*. New York: Academic Press, 1977. Print.

Lacan, Jacques. *The Four Fundamental Concepts of Psychoanalysis*. Ed. Jacques Alain Miller. Trans. Alan Sheridan. New York: Norton, 1981. Print.

———. *Écrits*. Trans. Bruce Fink. New York: Norton, 1996. Print.

Laclau, Ernesto and Chantal Mouffe. *Hegemony and Socialist Strategy: Towards a Radical Democratic Politics*. 1985. 2nd ed. London: Verso, 2001. Print.

Lakoff, George and Mark Johnson. *Metaphors We Live By*. Chicago: University of Chicago Press, 1980. Print.

Lakoff, Robin. "Language and Woman's Place." *Language in Society* 2.1 (1973): 45–80. Print. Published later as *Language and Woman's Place*. New York: Harper Collins, 1975. Print.

Leeuwen, Theo van. *Introducing Social Semiotics*. London: Routledge, 2004. Print.

Leslie, Alan M. "The Necessity of Illusion: Perception and Thought in Infancy." *Thought Without Language*. Ed. Lawrence Weiskrantz. Oxford: Clarendon Press, 1988. Print.

Bibliography 121

Levinson, Stephen C. *Pragmatics.* Cambridge: Cambridge University Press, 1983. Print.

Locke, Abigail and Derek Edwards. "Bill and Monica: Memory, Emotion and Normativity in Clinton's Grand Jury Testimony." *British Journal of Social Psychology* 42.0 (2003): 239–256. Print.

Lyotard, Jean François. *The Postmodern Condition: A Report on Knowledge.* 1979. Manchester: Manchester University Press, 1984. Print.

Markus, Hazel. "Self-Schemata and Processing Information about the Self." *Journal of Personality and Social Psychology* 35.2 (1977): 63–78. Print.

Marx, Karl and Frederic Engels. *The German Ideology.* London: Lawrence and Wishart, 1970. Print.

Martinez-Guzman, Antar, Marisela Montenegro, and Joan Pujol. "Towards a Situated Approach to Sex/Gender Identities." *Annual Review of Critical Psychology* 11.0 (2014): 1–21. Print.

Maslow, Abraham Harold. *Towards a Psychology of Being.* 2nd ed. Princeton: Van Nostrand, 1968. Print.

Massumi, Brian. "The Autonomy of Affect." *Cultural Critique* 31.0 (1995): 83–109. Print.

———. *Parables for the Virtual: Movements, Affect, Sensation.* Durham, NC: Duke University Press, 2002. Print.

Mills, Sara. *Feminist Stylistics.* London: Routledge, 1995. Print.

Molotch, Harvey L. and Deidre Boden. "Talking Social Structure: Discourse, Domination and The Watergate Hearings." *American Sociological Review* 50.0 (1985): 273–288. Print.

Moscovici, Serge. *Social Representations: Explorations in Social Psychology.* Ed. Gerard Duveen. Cambridge: Polity Press, 2000. Print.

Nayak, Suryia. *Race, Gender and the Activism of Black Feminist Theory. Working with Audre Lorde.* Abingdon and New York: Routledge, 2014. Print.

Neisser, Ulric. *Cognition and Reality.* San Francisco: W.H. Freeman and Company, 1976. Print.

Newman, Fred and Louis Holzman. "Against Against-ism: Comment on Parker." *Critical Discursive Psychology.* Ed. Ian Parker. Basingstoke, Hampshire: Palgrave Macmillan, 2015. 54–59. Print.

Paltridge, Brian. *Discourse Analysis: An Introduction.* London: Continuum, 2006.

Parker, Ian. "Discourse: Definitions and Contradictions." *Philosophical Psychology* 3.2–3 (1990a): 187–204. Rept. *Critical Discursive Psychology.* Ed. Ian Parker. Basingstoke, Hampshire: Palgrave Macmillan, 2015. 148–164. Print.

———. "Real Things: Discourse, Context and Practice." *Philosophical Psychology* 3.2–3 (1990b): 219–225. Print.

———. "Tracing Therapeutic Discourse in Material Culture." *Psychology and Psychotherapy: Theory, Research, Practice* 72.4 (1999): 577–587. Rept. *Critical Discursive Psychology.* Ed. Ian Parker. Basingstoke, Hampshire: Palgrave Macmillan, 2015. 209–223. Print.

———. *Qualitative Psychology: Introducing Radical Research.* Maidenhead, Berkshire: Open University Press, 2005a. Print.

———. "Lacanian Discourse Analysis in Psychology: Seven Theoretical Elements." *Theory and Psychology* 15.2 (2005b): 163–182. Print.

———. "Critical Psychology: What It Is and What It Is Not." *Social and Personality Psychology Compass* 1.1 (2007): 1–15. Print.

———. "Psychosocial Studies: Lacanian Discourse Analysis Negotiating Interview Text." *Psychoanalysis, Culture and Society* 15.2 (2010): 156–172. Print.

———. *Lacanian Psychoanalysis: Revolutions in Subjectivity.* East Sussex: Routledge, 2011. Print.

122 Bibliography

———. *Critical Discursive Psychology*. 2002. 2nd ed. Basingstoke, Hampshire: Palgrave Macmillan, 2015a. Print.

———. ed. *Handbook of Critical Psychology*. East Sussex: Routledge, 2015b. Print.

———. "Discursive Resources in the Discourse Unit." *Annual Review of Critical Psychology* 13.0 (2017): 1–13. Print.

Peräkylä, Anssi, et al., eds. *Conversation Analysis and Psychotherapy*. Cambridge: Cambridge University Press, 2008. Print.

Piaget, Jean. *The Origins of Intelligence in Children*. London: Routledge and Kegan Paul, 1952. Print.

Pomerantz, Anita. "Compliment Responses: Notes on the Cooperation of Multiple Constraints." *Studies in the Organization of Conversational Interaction*. Ed. Jim Schenkein. London: Academic Press, 1978. Print.

———. "Agreeing and Disagreeing with Assessments: Some Features of Preferred/ Dispreferred Turn Shapes." *Structures of Social Action: Studies in Conversation Analysis*. Ed. J. Maxwell Atkinson and John Heritage. Cambridge: Cambridge University Press, 1984. Print.

Pomerantz, Anita and John Heritage. "Preference." *The Handbook of Conversation Analysis*. Ed. Jack Sidnell and Tanya Stivers. London: Blackwell Publishing, 2012. 210–228. Print.

Potter, Jonathan. "Reading Repertoires: A Preliminary Study of Some Techniques That Scientists Use to Construct Readings." *Science and Technology Studies* 5.0 (1987): 112–121. Print.

———. *Representing Reality: Discourse, Rhetoric and Social Construction*. London: Sage, 1996. Print.

———. "Re-reading Discourse and Social Psychology: Transforming Social Psychology." *British Journal of Social Psychology* 51.3 (2012): 436–455. Print.

Potter, Jonathan and Derek Edwards. "Rethinking Cognition: On Coulter on Discourse and Mind." *Human Studies* 26.0 (2003): 165–181. Print.

———. "Conversation Analysis and Psychology." *The Handbook of Conversation Analysis*. Ed. Jack Sidnell and Tanya Stivers. London: Blackwell Publishing, 2012. 701–725. Print.

Potter, Jonathan, Derek Edwards, and Malcolm Ashmore. "Regulating Criticism: Some Comments on an Argumentative Complex." *History of the Human Sciences* 12.4 (1999): 79–88. Print.

Potter, Jonathan and Quentin Halliday. "Community Leaders as a Device for Warranting Versions of Crowd Events." *Journal of Pragmatics* 14.0 (1990): 725–741. Print.

Potter, Jonathan and Alexa Hepburn. "Discursive Psychology: Mind and Reality in Practice." *Language, Discourse and Social Psychology*. Ed. Ann Weatherall, Bernadette M. Watson, and Cindy Gallois. Basingstoke, Hampshire: Palgrave Macmillan, 2007. 160–181. Print.

Potter, Jonathan and Michael Mulkay. "Scientists' Interview Talk: Interview as a Technique for Revealing Participants' Interpretative Practices." *The Research Interview: Use and Approaches*. Ed. Michael Brenner, Jennifer Brown, and David Canter. London: Academic Press, 1985. Print.

Potter, Jonathan and Margaret Wetherell. *Discourse and Social Psychology: Beyond Attitudes and Behaviour*. London: Sage, 1987. Print.

———. "Accomplished Attitudes: Facts and Evaluation in Racist Talk." *Text* 8.0 (1988): 51–68. Print.

Potter, Jonathan, Margaret Wetherell, and Andrew Chitty. "Quantification Rhetoric – Cancer on Television." *Discourse and Society* 2.3 (1991): 333–365. Print.

Bibliography 123

Potter, Jonathan, Margaret Wetherell, Ros Gill, and Derek Edwards. "Discourse: Noun, Verb or Social Practice?" *Philosophical Psychology* 3.2 (1990): 205–217. Print.

Propp, Vladimir. *Morphology of the Folktale*. 1928. Trans. Laurence Scott. Rev. Louis A. Wagner. Austin: University of Texas Press, 1968. Print.

Puchta, Claudia and Jonathan Potter. "Manufacturing Individual Opinions: Market Research Focus Groups and the Discursive Psychology of Evaluation." *British Journal of Social Psychology* 41.0 (2002): 345–363. Print.

———. *Focus Group Practice*. London: Sage, 2004. Print.

Radley, Alan and Michael Billig. "Accounts of Health and Illness: Dilemmas and Representations." *Sociology of Health and Illness* 18.2 (1996): 220–240. Print.

Redman, Peter. "Once More with Feeling: What Is the Psychosocial Anyway?" *Journal of Psychosocial Studies* 9.1 (2016): 73–93. Print.

Rogers, Carl. *Client-Centered Therapy: Its Current Practice, Implications and Theory*. London: Constable, 1951. Print.

———. "The Necessary and Sufficient Conditions of Therapeutic Personality Change." *Journal of Consulting and Clinical Psychology* 21.0 (1957): 95–103. Print.

———. *On Becoming a Person*. Boston: Houghton Mifflin, 1961. Print.

Sacks, Harvey, Emanuel A. Schegloff, and Gail Jefferson. "A Simplest Systematics for the Organization of Turn-Taking for Conversation." *Language* 50.4 (1974): 696–735. Print.

Saussure, Ferdinand. *Course in General Linguistics*. 1915. Glasgow: Fontana and Collins, 1974. Print.

Schank, Roger C. and Robert P. Abelson. *Scripts, Plans, Goals and Understanding: An Inquiry into Human Knowledge Structures*. Hillsdale, NJ: Lawrence Erlbaum, 1977. Print.

Schegloff, Emanuel. "Whose Text? Whose Context?" *Discourse and Society* 8.2 (1997): 165–187. Print.

———. "On Integrity in Inquiry . . . of the Investigated, not the Investigator." *Discourse Studies* 7.4–5 (2005): 455–480. Print.

Schiffrin, Deborah. *Approaches to Discourse Analysis*. Oxford: Blackwell Publishing, 1994. Print.

Schneider, Peter. "Language Usage and Social Action in the Psychoanalytic Encounter: Discourse Analysis of a Therapy Session Fragment." *Language and Psychoanalysis* 2.1 (2013): 4–19. Print.

Searle, John. *Speech Acts*. Cambridge: Cambridge University Press, 1969. (Rept. 1974.) Print.

———. *Expressions and Meaning*. Cambridge: Cambridge University Press, 1979. Print.

Segal, Lynne. *Why Feminism?* Cambridge: Polity Press, 1999. Print.

Semino, Elena and Jonathan Culpeper, eds. *Cognitive Stylistics: Language and Cognition in Text Analysis*. Amsterdam: John Benjamins, 2002. Print.

Sharma, Saumya. "Students' Discourses about the Inclusion of Transgenders in Higher Education." *International Journal of Communication* (Bahri Publishers) 27.2 (2017): 100–118. Print.

———. *Language, Gender and Ideology: Constructions of Femininity for Marriage*. Abingdon, Oxon: Routledge, 2018. Print.

Shotter, John. *Conversational Realities: The Construction of Life Through Language*. London: Sage, 1993. Print.

———. "Rhetoric and Argumentation." *Rhetoric, Ideology and Social Psychology: Essays in Honour of Michael Billig*. Ed. Charles Antaki and Susan Condor. East Sussex: Routledge, 2014. 43–56. Print.

Sinclair, John McHardy and Malcolm Coulthard. *Towards an Analysis of Discourse: The English Used by Teachers and Pupils*. Oxford: Oxford University Press, 1975. Print.

124 Bibliography

Smith, Dorothy E. *Texts, Facts and Femininity: Exploring the Relations of Ruling*. 1990. London: Routledge, 1993. Online edition. Web. Access: 5 May 2015. Print.

Smith, Jean. "Self and Experience in Maori Culture." *Indigenous Psychologies: The Anthropology of the Self*. Ed. Paul Heelas and Andrew Lock. London: Academic Press, 1981. 145–160. Print.

Speer, Susan. "'Natural' and 'Contrived' Data: A Sustainable Distinction?" *Discourse Studies* 4.4 (2002): 511–525. Print.

Sperber, Dan and Deirdre Wilson. *Relevance: Communication and Cognition*. Oxford: Basil Blackwell, 1986. Print.

Stier, Jonas and Helena Blomberg. "The Quest for Truth: The Use of Discursive and Rhetorical Resources in Newspaper Coverage of the (Mis)treatment of Young Swedish Gymnasts." *Discourse and Communication* 10.1 (2015): 65–81. Print.

Strauss, Claude Lévi. *Structural Anthropology*. 1958. Trans. Claire Jacobson and Brooke Grundfest Schoepf. New York: Basil Books, 1963. Print.

Stubbs, Michael. *Discourse Analysis: The Sociolinguistic Analysis of Natural Language*. Chicago: University of Chicago Press, 1983. Print.

Talbot, Mary. "A Synthetic Sisterhood: False Friends in a Teenage Magazine." *Gender Articulated: Language and the Socially Constructed Self*. Ed. Kira Hall and Mary Bucholtz. New York: Routledge, 1995. 143–168. Print.

Tenbrink, Thora. "Cognitive Discourse Analysis: Accessing Cognitive Representations and Processes Through Language Data." *Language and Cognition* 7.0 (2015): 98–137. Print.

Tsui, Amy Bik May. "Beyond the Adjacency Pair." *Language in Society* 18.4 (1989): 545–564. Print.

———. *English Conversation*. Oxford: Oxford University Press, 1998. Print.

Turnbull, William. *Language in Action: Psychological Models of Conversation*. East Sussex: Psychology, 2003. Print.

Vaillant, George E. *Adaptation to Life*. Massachusetts: Harvard University Press, 1977. Print.

van Dijk, Teun A. *Prejudice in Discourse*. Amsterdam: Benjamins, 1984. Print.

———. "Introduction: Discourse Analysis as a New Cross Discipline." *Handbook of Discourse Analysis: Disciplines of Discourse*. Vol. 1. London: Academic, 1985. 1–10. Print.

———. *Communicating Racism: Ethnic Prejudice in Thought and Talk*. Newbury: Sage, 1987. Print.

———. *News as Discourse*. Hillsdale, NJ: Lawrence Erlbaum, 1988. Print.

———. *Racism and the Press*. London: Routledge, 1991a. Print.

———. "Editorial: Discourse Analysis with a Cause." *The Semiotic Review of Books* 2.1 (1991b): 1–2. Print.

———. "Ideological Discourse Analysis." *Special Issue Interdisciplinary Approaches to Discourse Analysis New Courant* 4 (1995): 135–161. Print.

———. ed. *Discourse as Structure and Process. Discourse Studies: A Multidisciplinary Introduction*. Vol. 1. London: Sage, 1997. Print.

———. *Ideology: A Multidisciplinary Approach*. London: Sage, 1998. Print.

———. "Discourse and Manipulation." *Discourse and Society* 17.3 (2006): 359–383. Print.

———. *Discourse and Context: A Sociocognitive Approach*. Cambridge: Cambridge University Press, 2008a. Print.

———. *Discourse and Power*. Basingstoke, Hampshire: Palgrave Macmillan, 2008b. Print.

———. *Society and Discourse: How Social Contexts Influence Text and Talk*. Cambridge: Cambridge University Press, 2009. Print.

———. "Critical Discourse Studies: A Sociocognitive Approach." *Methods of Critical Discourse Studies*. Ed. Ruth Wodak and Michael Meyer. 3rd ed. London: Sage, 2016. Print.

Bibliography **125**

van Dijk, Teun A. and Walter Kintsch. *Strategies of Discourse Comprehension.* New York: Academic Press, 1983. Print.

Vološinov, Valentin Nikolaevich. "Language as Dialogic Interaction." 1973. *The Bakhtin Reader.* Ed. Pam Morris. Comp. Graham Roberts. London: Arnold, 1994. 48–60. Print.

Walkerdine, Valerie. *The Mastery of Reason.* London: Routledge and Keagan Paul, 1988. Print.

————. *Schoolgirl Fictions.* London: Verso, 1990. Print.

Weiss, Gilbert and Ruth Wodak, eds. *Critical Discourse Analysis: Theory and Interdisciplinarity.* New York: Palgrave Macmillan, 2003. Print.

Wetherell, Margaret. "Positioning and Interpretative Repertoires: Conversation Analysis and Post-structuralism in Dialogue." *Discourse and Society* 9.0 (1998): 387–412. Print.

————. "Subjectivity or Psycho-Discursive Practices? Investigating Complex Intersectional Identities." *Subjectivity* 22.1 (2008): 73–81. Print.

————. *Affect and Emotion: A New Social Science Understanding.* London: Sage, 2012. Print.

————. "Affect and Discourse – What's the Problem? From Affect as Excess to Affective/Discursive Practice." *Subjectivity* 6.4 (2013): 349–368. Print.

Wetherell, Margaret and Nigel Edley. "Jockeying for Position: The Construction of Masculine Identities." *Discourse and Society* 8.2 (1997): 203–217. Print.

————. "Negotiating Hegemonic Masculinity: Imaginary Positions and Psycho-Discursive Practices." *Feminism and Psychology* 9.3 (1999): 335–356. Print.

————. "A Discursive Psychological Framework for Analysing Men and Masculinities." *Psychology of Men and Masculinity* 15.4 (2014): 355–364. Print.

Wetherell, Margaret and Jonathan Potter. "Discourse Analysis and the Identification of Interpretative Repertoires." *Analysing Everyday Explanation: A Casebook of Methods.* Ed. Charles Antaki. Thousand Oaks, CA: Sage, 1988. 168–83. Print.

Wetherell, Margaret, Stephanie Taylor, and Simeon J. Yates, eds. *Discourse Theory and Practice: A Reader.* London: Sage, 2001. Print.

Widdowson, Henry G. *Text, Context and Pretext: Critical Issues in Discourse Analysis.* Oxford: Blackwell Publishing, 2004. Print.

Wierzbicka, Anna. *Semantics, Culture and Cognition: Universal Human Concepts in Culture-Specific Configurations.* Oxford: Oxford University Press, 1992. Print.

"Wife Hammers Navy Staff to Death in Goa after Years of Domestic Abuse, Say Cops." *Hindustan Times* 2 June 2019. Panaji, Goa. Web Access: 10 June 2019. www.hindustantimes.com; https://www.hindustantimes.com/india-news/wife-hammers-navy-staffer-to-death-in-goa-after-years-of-domestic-abuse-say-cops/story-mVL52 dYKsck2PJ6OuE63jL.html

Wiggins, Sally. *Discursive Psychology: Theory, Method and Applications.* London: Sage, 2017. Print.

Wiggins, Sally and Jonathan Potter. "Discursive Psychology." *Handbook of Qualitative Research in Psychology.* Ed. Carla Willig and Wendy Rogers. London: Sage, 2017. 73–90. Print.

Wittgenstein, Ludwig. *Philosophical Investigations.* London: Blackwell Publishing, 1953. Print.

Wodak Ruth. "Turning the Tables: Antisemitic Discourse in Post-war Austria." *Discourse and Society* 2.1 (1991): 65–83. Print.

————. *Disorders of Discourse.* London: Longman, 1996. Print.

————. ed. *Gender and Discourse.* London: Sage, 1997. Print.

Wodak, Ruth and Bernd Matouschek. "We Are Dealing with People Whose Origins One Can Clearly Tell Just by Looking: Critical Discourse Analysis and the Study of Neoracism in Contemporary Austria." *Discourse and Society* 4.2 (1993): 225–248. Print.

126 Bibliography

Wodak, Ruth and Michael Meyer, eds. *Methods of Critical Discourse Analysis*. 3rd ed. London: Sage, 2016. Print.

Wooffitt, Robin. *Telling Tales of the Unexpected: The Organization of Factual Discourse*. Savage, MD: Barnes and Noble Books, 1992. Print.

Young, Lisa Saville and Stephen Frosh. "Discourse and Psychoanalysis: Translating Concepts into 'Fragmenting' Methodology." *Psychology in Society* 28.0 (2009): 1–16. Print.

———. "And Where Were Your Brothers in All This? A Psychosocial Approach to Texts on Brothering." *Qualitative Research* 10.5 (2010): 511–531. Print.

Žižek, Slavoj. *The Sublime Object of Ideology*. London: Verso, 1989. Print.

———. *The Metastases of Enjoyment*. London: Verso, 1994. Print.

———. *The Ticklish Subject*. London: Verso, 2000. Print.

INDEX

Abelson, R. *see* schemas, scripts
accountability *see* attribution
Althusser, L. 20, 68–69; *see also* ideology
argumentative thinking 64–66; analysis 94–98; analysis of arguments 66–68
Aristotle 63–68
attitudes 7, 49–53
attribution 38, 40–41, 109; *see also* discursive action model (DAM)
Austin, J. 5

Bakhtin, M. 13
Barthes, R. 4
beliefs 14; *see also* context, models
Billig, M. 7, 63–73, 107–108; analysis 94
Brown, G. 9
Brown, P. 5

Cap, P. 34
categorization 46–48; *see also* out-there-ness
category entitlement *see* categorization; discursive action model (DAM)
Chomsky, N. *see* cognitivism
cognitivism 37–38
cognitive discourse analysis 111
cognitive language approach 33–34
community *see* racism
Connell, R. W. 75–77
conversational maxims *see* implicature
conversation analysis 6, 10, 51; *see also* discursive psychology
context 15, 17–19; discursive features 26–27; models 17–22; and social cognition 22–24

corpus-assisted discourse analysis 14–15
co-text 15
Coulthard, M. 6, 10
critical discourse analysis (CDA) 6–7, 11, 17, 20, 59–61, 88–89
critical linguistics 11
critical psychology concepts 80–82; analysis 104–106; critical realism and postmodernism 82–85; discourse analysis 85–87; Lacan and discourse 87–88
Culpeper, J. 5, 109

dialogic unconscious 71–73
Dijk, T. A. van 3–4, 6–7, 17–29, 88–89, 107–108; analysis 99–101
discourse analysis: Foucauldian discourse 12–13; linguistic meanings of discourse 8–12; news discourse 27–28; origins of discourse analysis 3–8; scope 14–15
discursive action model (DAM) 44–48; analysis 94–98
discursive psychology 7; basic issues 36–37; conversation analysis 43–44; discourse and social psychology 49–51; language 37–38; meaning of discourse 42–43; psychological states/ themes 38–41; Potter and Wetherell's methodology 56–58

Edley, N. 57–59
Edwards, D. 36–48; analysis 93–94
Emerson, P. 8, 78–79, 109
emotion 39–41, 74–75; *see also* discursive psychology, states/themes; psycho-discursive practices

128 Index

Engels, F. 68–69
ethnomethodology 6; *see also* conversation analysis
experience models 18; *see also* context, models

Fairclough, N. 5–7, 24
Fasulo, A. 41
Fauconnier, G. 30
femininity 91–94, 102–103
feminism 69–70
footing 47–48
Foucault, M. 12, 74–75; *see also* power
Fowler, R. 11
Freud, S. *see* dialogic unconscious
Frosh, S. 8, 74–80, 109; analysis 101–104

Gee, J. P. 79–80; analysis 101–104
genre 21–22, 26
Gilbert, N. 53–55
Gill, R. 91–92
Goffman, E. 4–6; *see also* footing
grammar 5–6; *see also* grammatica
grammatica 3
Grice, H. P. 5, 10

Halliday, M. A. K. 5, 9–10
Harris, Z. 8
Hart, C. 33–34, 108
Holland, N. 109–110
Hymes, D. 4

ideology 20, 24–26, 52–53, 57–58, 96; analysis 104–106; ideological dilemmas 68–70; types of ideology 70–71; *see also* critical psychology concepts, critical realism; psychosocial studies objectives
implicature 5, 10
impoliteness 5, 109; *see also* dialogic unconscious
impression formation 109
interpretative repertoires 53–55; analysis 91–94; *see also* discursive psychology, Potter and Wetherell's methodology; psycho-discursive practices; sexuality
intersubjectivity 40–41
intertextuality 12–13
introjection 102–103

Jefferson, G. 6, 18, 43; *see also* conversation analysis
Johnson, M. 29–30

Koller, V. 30–33, 107–108

Labov, W. 4
Lacan, J. 87–88; *see also* critical psychology; psychosocial studies objectives
Lakoff, G. 29–30
Lakoff, R. 69
language and psychotherapy 110–111
Levinson, S. 5
Lincoln, A. 99–101
Locke, A. 39

Marx, K. 68–69
masculinity 57–59; *see also* psychosocial studies objectives, masculinity studies
media analysis 91–93, 98–99
memory 14; *see also* discursive action model (DAM); discursive psychology, psychological states/themes
metaphor 29; blending theory 30–31; conceptual metaphor theory 29–30; sociocognitive representations 32–33
Mulkay, M. 53–55

narrative 3; analysis 94–98, 101–104; *see also* discursive action model (DAM); psychosocial studies objectives

out-there-ness 59–61

Parker, I. 7, 80–88
Pattman, R. 75–77
Phoenix, A. 75–77
politeness 5, 26; *see also* dialogic unconscious
poststructuralism 57–58
Potter, J. 7, 36–48, 49–61; analysis 91–94
power 12–13, 24–26, 74–75, 79–80, 80–82; analysis 104–106; *see also* critical psychology concepts, critical realism; discourse analysis
presuppositions 26
Propp, V. 4
psychoanalysis 80–82, 107–108; *see also* dialogic unconscious, psychosocial studies objectives; language and psychotherapy
psycho-discursive practices 58–59
psychosocial studies objectives 74–75; analysis 101–104; masculinity studies 75–77; narrative, psychoanalysis and discourse 77–80

racism 28–29, 52, 55–56
Radley, A. 71, 94

reader-response theory 109–110
reflexivity 50
rhetoric 3; *see also* rhetorical psychology
rhetorical psychology 63–68
repression *see* dialogic unconscious
role theory 51–52

Sacks, H. 6, 18, 43; *see also* conversation analysis
Schank, R. *see* schemas, scripts
Schegloff, E. 6, 18, 43; *see also* conversation analysis
schemas 14, 20–23, 33–34, 70; scripts 38–39; *see also* discursive action model (DAM); discursive psychology, psychological states/themes
Searle, J. 5
self 23–24; *see also* subjectivity
sexuality 57–59; *see also* masculinity
shared knowledge 20–23
Sharma, S. 92–94
Shotter, J. 7, 65
Sinclair, J. 6, 10
sociocognitive approach 14, 99–101; *see also* cognitive language approach; context, models; metaphor

speech acts 5
Speer, S. 93
Sperber, D. 5
stereotypes *see* racism
subjectivity 51–53, 77–80
systemic functional linguistics 5, 9–10
systemic functional linguistics *see* Halliday, M. A. K.

Tenbrink, T. 111
text 8–10
trait theory 51
triangulation approach 20
Turner, M. 30

variability 50

Wetherell, M. 7, 49–61; analysis 91–93
Widdowson, H. G. 9
Wilson, D. 5
Wodak, R. 6, 24

Young, L. S. 77
Yule, G. 9

Žižek, S. 74–75, 77–79, 87–88

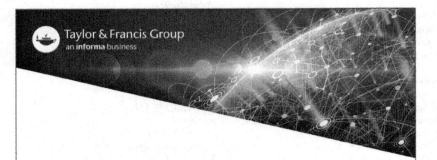